Cedar

Please treat
save this book, it is 123
years old.

SHAKESPEARE AT THE AGE OF TWELVE

From the painting by J. Sant

SHAKESPEARE THE BOY

WITH SKETCHES OF
THE HOME AND SCHOOL LIFE, THE GAMES
AND SPORTS, THE MANNERS, CUSTOMS
AND FOLK-LORE OF THE TIME

BY

WILLIAM J. ROLFE, Litt.D.

ILLUSTRATED

NEW YORK AND LONDON
HARPER & BROTHERS PUBLISHERS

PREFACE

Two years ago, at the request of the editors of the *Youth's Companion*, I wrote for that periodical a series of four familiar articles on the boyhood of Shakespeare. It was understood at the time that I might afterwards expand them into a book, and this plan is carried out in the present volume. The papers have been carefully revised and enlarged to thrice their original compass, and a new fifth chapter has been added.

The sources from which I have drawn my material are often mentioned in the text and the notes. I have been particularly indebted to Halliwell-Phillipps's *Outlines of the Life of Shakespeare*, Knight's *Biography of Shakspere*, Furnivall's Introduction to the "Leopold" edition of Shakespeare, his *Babees Book*, and his edition of Harrison's *Description of England*, Sidney Lee's *Stratford-on-Avon*, Strutt's *Sports and Pastimes*, Brand's *Popular Antiquities*, and Dyer's *Folk-Lore of Shakespeare*.

I hope that the book may serve to give the young folk some glimpses of rural life in England when Shakespeare was a boy, and also to help them—and possibly their elders—to a better understanding of many allusions in his works.

W. J R.

CAMBRIDGE, *June* 10, 1896.

CONTENTS

ILLUSTRATIONS

SHAKESPEARE THE BOY

PART I
HIS NATIVE TOWN AND NEIGHBORHOOD

WARWICKSHIRE

THE county of Warwick was called the heart of England as long ago as the time of Shakespeare. Indeed, it was his friend, Michael Drayton, born the year before himself, who first called it so. In his *Poly-Olbion* (1613) Drayton refers to his native county as "That shire which we the heart of England well may call." The form of the expression seems to imply that it was original with him. It was doubtless suggested by the central situation of the county, about equidistant from the eastern, western, and southern shores of the island; but it is no less appropriate with reference to its historical, romantic, and poetical associations. Drayton, whose rhymed geography in the *Poly-Olbion* is rather prosaic and tedious, attains a kind of genuine inspiration when, in his 13th book, he comes to describe

" Brave Warwick that abroad so long advanced her Bear,
  By her illustrious Earls renowned everywhere;
  Above her neighboring shires which always bore her
  head."

The verse catches something of the music of the throstle and the lark, of the woosel " with golden bill " and the nightingale with her tender strains, as he tells of these Warwickshire birds, and of the region with " flowery bosom brave " where they breed and warble; but in Shakespeare the same birds sing with a finer music —more like that to which we may still listen in the fields and woodlands along the lazy-winding Avon.

WARWICK CASTLE AND SAINT MARY'S CHURCH.

Warwickshire is the heart of England, and the country within ten miles or so of the town of Warwick may be called the heart of this heart. On one side of this circle are Stratford and Shottery and Wilmcote — the home of Shakespeare's mother—and on the other are Kenilworth and Coventry.

In Warwick itself is the famous castle of its Earls— " that fairest monument," as Scott calls it, "of ancient and chivalrous splendor which yet remains uninjured by time." The earlier description written by the veracious Dugdale almost two hundred and fifty years ago might be applied to it to-day. It is still " not only a place of great strength, but extraordinary delight; with most pleasant gardens, walls, and thickets such as this part of England can hardly parallel; so that now it is the most princely seat that is within the midland parts of this realm."

The castle was old in Shakespeare's day. Cæsar's Tower, so called, though not built, as tradition alleged, by the mighty Julius, dated back to an unknown period;

WARWICK CASTLE

and Guy's Tower, named in honor of the redoubted Guy of Warwick, the hero of many legendary exploits, was built in 1394. No doubt the general appearance of the buildings was more ancient in the sixteenth century than it is to-day, for they had been allowed to become somewhat dilapidated; and it was not until the reign of James I. that they were repaired and embel-

lished, at enormous expense, and made the stately fortress and mansion that Dugdale describes.

But the castle would be no less beautiful for situation, though it were fallen to ruin like the neighboring
Kenilworth. The rock on which it stands, washed at
its base by the Avon, would still be there, the park
would still stretch its woods and glades along the river,
and all the natural attractions of the noble estate would
remain.

We cannot doubt that the youthful Shakespeare was
familiar with the locality.   Warwick and Kenilworth
were probably the only baronial castles he had seen
before he went to London ; and, whatever others he
may have seen later in life, these must have continued
to be his ideal castles as in his boyhood.

It is not likely that he was ever in Scotland, and
when he described the castle of Macbeth the picture
in his mind's eye was doubtless Warwick or Kenilworth,
and more likely the former than the latter ; for

" *This* castle hath a pleasant seat ; the air
  Nimbly and sweetly recommends itself
  Unto our gentle senses. This guest of summer,
  The temple-haunting martlet, does approve,
  By his loved mansionry, that the air
  Smells wooingly here ; no jutty, frieze,
  Buttress, nor coign of vantage, but this bird
  Hath made his pendent bed and procreant cradle.
  Where they most breed and haunt I have observed
  The air is delicate."

Saint Mary's church at Warwick was also standing
then—the most interesting church in Warwickshire next
to Holy Trinity at Stratford. It was burned in 1694,

but the beautiful choir and the magnificent lady chapel, or Beauchamp Chapel, fortunately escaped the flames, and we see them to-day as Shakespeare doubtless saw them, except for the monuments that have since been added. *He* saw in the choir the splendid tomb of Thomas Beauchamp, Earl of Warwick, and in the adjacent chapel the grander tomb of Richard Beauchamp, unsurpassed in the kingdom except by that of Henry VII. in Westminster Abbey. *He* looked, as we do, on the full-length figure of the Earl, recumbent in armor of gilded brass, under the herse of brass hoops also gilt ; his hands elevated in prayer, the garter on his left knee, the swan at his head, the griffin and bear at his feet. *He* read, as we read, in the inscription on the cornice of the sepulchre, how this " most worshipful knight decessed full christenly the last day of April the year of oure Lord God 1439, he being at that time lieutenant general and governor of the realm of Fraunce," and how his body was brought to Warwick, and " laid with full solemn exequies in a fair chest made of stone in this church " on the 4th day of October—" honoured be God therefor." And the young Shakespeare looked up, as we do, at the exquisitely carved stone ceiling, and at the great east window, which still contains the original glass, now almost four and a half centuries old, with the portrait of Earl Richard kneeling in armor with upraised hands.

The tomb of " the noble Impe, Robert of Dudley," who died in 1584, with the lovely figure of a child seven or eight years old, may have been seen by Shakespeare when he returned to Stratford in his latter years, and also the splendid monument of the father of the " noble imp," Robert Dudley, the great Earl of Leicester, who

died in 1588; but in the poet's youth this famous nobleman was living in the height of his renown and prosperity at the castle of Kenilworth five miles away, which
we will visit later.

WARWICK IN HISTORY.

Only brief reference can be made here to the important part that Warwick, or its famous Earl, Richard
Neville, the " King-maker," played in the English history on which Shakespeare founded several dramas,
—the three Parts of *Henry VI.* and *Richard III.* He
is the most conspicuous personage of those troublous
times. He had already distinguished himself by deeds
of bravery in the Scottish wars, before his marriage
with Anne, daughter and heiress of Richard Beauchamp, made him the most powerful nobleman in the
kingdom. By this alliance he acquired the vast estates
of the Warwick family, and became Earl of Warwick,
with the right to hand down the title to his descendants.
The immense revenues from his patrimony were aug-
mented by the income he derived from his various high
offices in the state; but his wealth was scattered with
a royal liberality. It is said that he daily fed thirty
thousand people at his numerous mansions.

The Lady Anne of *Richard III.*, whom the hero of
the play wooes in such novel fashion, was the youngest
daughter of the King-maker, born at Warwick Castle in
1452. Richard says, in his soliloquy at the end of the
first scene of the play :—

" I'll marry Warwick's youngest daughter.
What though I kill'd her husband and her father ?"

Her husband was Edward, Prince of Wales, son of Henry VI., and was slain at the battle of Tewkesbury.

The Earl of Warwick who figures in 2 *Henry IV.* was the Richard Beauchamp already mentioned as the father of Anne who became the wife of the King-maker. He appears again in the play of *Henry V.*, and also in the first scene of *Henry VI.*, though he has nothing to say; and, as some believe, he (and not his son) is the Earl of Warwick in the rest of the play, in spite of certain historical difficulties which that theory involves. In 2 *Henry IV.* (iii. 1. 66) Shakespeare makes the mistake of calling him "Nevil" instead of Beauchamp.

The title of the Warwick earls became extinct with the death of the King-maker on the battle-field of Barnet. It was then bestowed on George, Duke of Clarence, who was drowned in the butt of wine by order of his loving brother Richard. It then passed to the young son of Clarence, who is another character in the play of *Richard III.* He, like his unfortunate father, was long imprisoned in the Tower, and ultimately murdered there after the farce of a trial on account of his alleged complicity in a plot against Henry VII. The subsequent vicissitudes of the earldom do not appear in the pages of Shakespeare, and we will not refer to them here.

GUY OF WARWICK.

The dramatist was evidently familiar with the legendary renown of Warwick as well as its authentic history. Doubtless he had heard the story of the famous Guy of Warwick in his boyhood; and later he probably visited "Guy's Cliff," on the edge of the town of Warwick, where the hero is said to have spent the closing years of his life. Learned antiquarians, in these latter days, have proved that his adventures are mythical, but the common people believe in him as of old. There is his " cave " in the side of the " cliff " on the bank of the Avon, and his gigantic statue in the so-called chapel; and can we not see his sword, shield, and breastplate, his helmet and walking-staff, in the great hall of War-wick Castle? The breastplate alone weighs more than fifty pounds, and who but the mighty Guy could have worn it? There too is his porridge-pot of metal, hold-ing more than a hundred gallons, and the flesh-fork to match. We may likewise see a rib and other remains of the famous " dun cow," which he slew after the beast had long been the terror of the country round about. Unbelieving scientists doubt the bovine origin of these interesting relics, to be sure, as they doubt the existence of the stalwart destroyer of the animal; but the vulgar faith in them is not to be shaken.

Of Guy's many exploits the most noted was his con-flict with a gigantic Saracen, Colbrand by name, who was fighting with the Danes against Athelstan in the tenth century, and was slain by Guy, as the old ballad narrates. Subsequently Guy went on a pilgrimage to the Holy Land, leaving his wife in charge of his castle. Years passed, and he did not return. Meanwhile his lady lived an exemplary life, and from time to time be-stowed her alms on a poor pilgrim who had made his appearance at a secluded cell by the Avon, not far from the castle. She may sometimes have talked with him about her husband, whom she now gave up as lost, as-suming that he had perished by the fever of the East or the sword of the infidel. At last she received a sum-mons to visit the aged pilgrim on his death-bed, when, to her astonishment, he revealed himself as the long-lost Guy. In his early days, when he was wooing the lady, she had refused to give him her hand unless he performed certain deeds of prowess. These had not been accomplished without sins that weighed upon his conscience during his absence in Palestine; and he had made a vow to lead a monastic life after his return to his native land.

The legend, like others of the kind, was repeated in varied forms; and, according to one of these, when Guy came back to Warwick he begged alms at the gate of his castle. His wife did not recognize him, and he took this as a sign that the wrath of Heaven was not yet appeased. Thereupon he withdrew to the cell in the cliff, and did not make himself known to his wife until he was at the point of death.

Shakespeare refers to Guy in *Henry VIII.* (v. 4. 22), where a man exclaims, " I am not Samson, nor Sir Guy, nor Colbrand"; and Colbrand is mentioned again in *King John* (i. 1. 225) as " Colbrand the giant, that same mighty man."

The scene of Guy's legendary retreat on the bank of the Avon is a charming spot, and there was certainly a hermitage here at a very early period. Richard Beauchamp founded a chantry for two priests in 1422, and left directions in his will for rebuilding the chapel and setting up the statue of Guy in it. At the dissolution of the monasteries in the time of Henry VIII. the chapel and its possessions were bestowed upon a gentleman named Flammock, and the place has been a private residence ever since, though the present mansion was not built until the beginning of the eighteenth century. There is an ancient mill on the Avon not far from the house, commanding a beautiful view of the river and the cliff. The celebrated actress, Mrs. Siddons, lived for some time at Guy's Cliff as waiting-maid to Lady Mary Greatheed, whose husband built the mansion.

KENILWORTH CASTLE.

But we must now go on to Kenilworth, though we cannot linger long within its dilapidated walls, majestic even in ruin. If, as Scott says, Warwick is the finest example of its kind yet uninjured by time and kept up as a noble residence, Kenilworth is the most stupendous of similar structures that have fallen to decay. It was ancient in Shakespeare's day, having been originally built at the end of the eleventh century. Two hundred years later, in 1266, it was held for six months by the rebellious barons against Henry III. After having passed through sundry hands and undergone divers vicissitudes of fortune, it was given by Elizabeth to Robert Dudley, Earl of Leicester, who spent, in enlarging and adorning it, the enormous sum of £60,000 —three hundred thousand dollars, equivalent to at least two millions now. Scott, in his novel of *Kenilworth*, describes it, with no exaggeration of romance—for exaggeration would hardly be possible—as it was then. Its very gate-house, still standing complete, was, as Scott says, "equal in extent and superior in architecture to the baronial castle of many a northern chief"; but this was the mere portal of the majestic structure, enclosing seven acres with its walls, equally impregnable as a fortress and magnificent as a palace.

There were great doings at this castle of Kenilworth in 1575, when Shakespeare was eleven years old, and the good people from all the country roundabout thronged to see them. Then it was that Queen Elizabeth was entertained by Robert Dudley, Earl of Leicester, and from July 9th to July 27th there was a succession of holiday pageants in the most sumptuous and elaborate

GATE-HOUSE OF KENILWORTH CASTLE

style of the time. Master Robert Laneham, whose accuracy as a chronicler is not to be doubted, though he may have been, as Scott calls him, " as great a coxcomb as ever blotted paper," mentions, as a proof of the earl's hospitality, that " the clock bell rang not a note all the while her highness was there; the clock stood also still withal; the hands stood firm and fast, always pointing at two o'clock," the hour of banquet! The quantity of beer drunk on the occasion was 320 hogsheads, and the total expense of the entertainments is said to have been £1000 ($5000) a day.

John Shakespeare, as a well-to-do citizen of Stratford, would be likely to see something of that stately show, and it is not improbable that he took his son William with him. The description in the *Midsummer-Night's Dream* (ii. 1. 150) of

> "a mermaid on a dolphin's back
> Uttering such dulcet and harmonious sounds
> That the rude sea grew civil at her song,"

appears to be a reminiscence of certain features of the Kenilworth pageant. The minstrel Arion figured there, on a dolphin's back, singing of course ; and Triton, in the likeness of a mermaid, commanded the waves to be still ; and among the fireworks there were shooting-stars that fell into the water, like the stars that, as Oberon adds,

> "shot madly from their spheres
> To hear the sea-maid's music."

When Shakespeare was writing that early play, with its scenes in fairy-land, what more natural than that this youthful visit to what must then have seemed veritable fairy-land should recur to his memory and blend with the creations of his fancy ?

COVENTRY.

The road from Warwick to Kenilworth is one of the loveliest in England ; and that from Kenilworth five

COVENTRY CHURCHES AND PAGEANT

miles further on to Coventry is acknowledged to be *the* most beautiful in the kingdom ; yet it is only a different kind of beauty from the other, as that is from the beauty of the road between Warwick and Stratford.

Till you reach Kenilworth you have all the varieties of charming rural scenery — hill and dale, field and forest, river-bank and village, hall and castle and church, grouping themselves in ever-changing pictures of beauty and grandeur; and now you come to a straight road for nearly five miles, bordered on both sides by a double line of stately elms and sycamores, as impressive in its regularity as the preceding stretch had been in its kaleidoscopic mutations.

This magnificent avenue with its over-arching foliage brings us to Coventry, no mean city in our day, but retaining only a remnant of its ancient glory, In the time of Shakespeare it was the third city in the realm— the " Prince's Chamber," as it was called—unrivalled in the splendor of its monastic institutions, "full of associations of regal state and chivalry and high events."

In 1397 it had been the scene of the famous hostile meeting between Henry Bolingbroke, Duke of Hereford (afterwards Henry IV.), and Thomas Mowbray, Duke of Norfolk, which Shakespeare has immortalized in *Richard II.* Later Henry IV. held more than one parliament here ; and the city was often visited and honored with many marks of favor by Henry VI. and his queen, as also by Richard III., Henry VII., Elizabeth, and James I.

Coventry, moreover, played an important part in the history of the English Drama. It was renowned for the religious plays performed by the Grey Friars of its great monastery, and kept up, though with diminished

pomp, even after the dissolution of their establishment.
It was not until 1580 that these pageants were entirely
suppressed; and Shakespeare, who was then sixteen
years old, may have been an eye-witness of the latest
of them. No doubt he heard stories of their attractions
in former times, when, as we are told by Dugdale, they
were "acted with mighty state and reverence by the
friars of this house, had theatres for the several scenes,
very large and high, placed upon wheels, and drawn to
all the eminent parts of the city for the better advantage of spectators; and contained the story of the New
Testament composed into old English rhyme." There
were forty-three of these ancient plays, performed by the
monks until, as Tennyson puts it,

> "Bluff Harry broke into the spence,
> And turned the cowls adrift."

When the boy Shakespeare saw them — if he did see
them—they were played by the different guilds, or associations of tradespeople. Thus the Nativity and the
Offering of the Magi, with the Flight into Egypt and
the Slaughter of the Innocents, were rendered by the
company of Shearmen and Tailors; the Smiths' pageant was the Crucifixion; that of the Cappers was the
Resurrection; and so on. The account-books of the
guilds are still extant, with charges for helmets for
Herod and gear for his wife, for a beard for Judas and
the rope to hang him, etc. In the accounts of the
Drapers, whose pageant was the Last Judgment, we
find outlays for a "link to set the world on fire," "the
barrel for the earthquake," and kindred stage "properties."

In the books of the Smiths or Armorers, some of the charges are as follows:—

"*Item*, paid for v. schepskens for gods cote and for makyng, iii*s*.

Item, paid for mendyng of Herods hed and a myter and other thyngs, ii*s*.

Item, paid for dressyng of the devells hede, viii*d*.

Item, paid for a pair of gloves for god, ii*d*."

The most elaborate and costly of the properties was "Hell-Mouth," which was used in several plays, but specially in the representation of the Last Judgment. This was a huge and grotesque head of canvas, with vast gaping mouth armed with fangs and vomiting flames. The jaws were made to open and shut, and through them the Devil made his entrance and the lost souls their exit. The making and repairing of this was a constant expense, and frequent entries like the following occur in the books of the guilds:—

"Paide for making and painting hell mouth, xii*d*.

Paid for keping of fyer at hell mouthe, iiii*d*."

Many curious details of the actors' dresses have come down to us. The representative of Christ wore a coat of white leather, painted and gilded, and a gilt wig. King Herod wore a mask and a helmet, sometimes of iron, adorned with gold and silver foil, and bore a sword and a sceptre. He was a very important character, and the manner in which he blustered and raged about the stage became proverbial. In *Hamlet* (iii. 2. 16) we have the expression, "It out-herods Herod"; and in the *Merry Wives of Windsor* (ii. 1. 20), "What a Herod of Jewry is this!"

All the actors were paid for their services, the amount varying with the importance of the part. The same actor, as in the theatres of Shakespeare's day, often played several parts. In addition to the payment of money, there was a plentiful supply of refreshments, especially of ale, for the actors. Pilate, who received the highest pay of the company, was moreover allowed wine instead of ale during the performance.

Reference has been made above to the "lost souls" in connection with Hell-Mouth. There were also "saved souls," who were dressed in white, as the lost were in black, or black and yellow. There is an allusion to the latter in *Henry V.* (ii. 3. 43), where the flea on Bardolph's rubicund nose is compared to "a black soul burning in hell-fire."

The Devil wore a dress of black leather, with a mask, and carried a club, with which he laid about him vigorously. His clothes were often covered with feathers or horsehair, to give him a shaggy appearance; and the traditional horns, tail, and cloven feet were sometimes added.

The regular time for these religious pageants was Corpus Christi Day, or the Thursday after Trinity Sunday, but they were occasionally performed on other days, especially at the time of a royal visit to Coventry, like that of Queen Margaret in 1455. Prince Edward was thus greeted in 1474, Prince Arthur in 1498, Henry VIII. in 1510, and Queen Elizabeth in 1565.

Shakespeare has other allusions to these old plays besides those here mentioned, showing that he knew them by report if he had not seen them.

Historical pageants, not Biblical in subject, were also familiar to the good people of Coventry a century at least before the dramatist was born. "The Nine Worthies," which he has burlesqued in *Love's Labour's Lost*, was acted there before Henry VI. and his queen in 1455. The original text of the play has been preserved, and portions of Shakespeare's travesty seem almost like a parody of it.

But we must not linger in the shadow of the "three tall spires" of Coventry, nor make more than a brief allusion to the legend of Godiva, the lady who rode naked through the town to save the people from a burdensome tax. It was an old story in Shakespeare's time, if, indeed, it had not been dramatized, like other chapters in the mythic annals of the venerable city. It has been proved to be without historical foundation, being mentioned by no writer before the fourteenth century, though the Earl who figures in the tale lived in the latter part of the eleventh century. The Benedictine Priory in Coventry, of which some fragments still remain, is said to have been founded by him in 1043. He died in 1057, and both he and his lady were buried in the porch of the monastery.

The effigy of "Peeping Tom" is still to be seen in the upper part of a house at the corner of Hertford Street in Coventry.

Shakespeare makes no reference to this story of Lady Godiva, though it was probably well known to him.

CHARLECOTE HALL.

Returning to Warwick, and travelling eight miles on the other side of the town, we come to Stratford. By one of the two roads we may take we pass Charlecote Hall and Park, associated with the tradition of Shakespeare's deer-poaching—a fine old mansion, seen across a breadth of fields dotted with tall elms.

The winding Avon skirts the enclosure to the west. The house, which has been in the possession of the Lucy family ever since the days of Shakespeare, stands at the water's edge. It has been enlarged in recent times, but the original structure has undergone no material change. It was begun in 1558, the year when

CHARLECOTE HALL

Elizabeth came to the throne, and was probably finished in 1559. It took the place of a much older mansion of which no trace remains, the ancestors of Sir Thomas Lucy having then held the estate for more than five centuries. The ground plan of the house is in the form of a capital letter E, being so arranged as a compliment to the Virgin Queen; and only one out of many such tributes paid her by noble builders of the time.

Over the main door are the royal arms, with the letters
E. R., together with the initials of the owner, T. L.

Within there is little to remind one of the olden time,
but some of the furniture of the library,—chairs, couch,
and cabinet of coromandel-wood inlaid with ivory,—is
said to have been presented by Elizabeth to Leicester
in 1575, and to have been brought from Kenilworth in
the seventeenth century. There is a modern bust of
Shakespeare in the hall.

The tradition that the dramatist in his youth was
guilty of deer-stealing in Sir Thomas's park is not improbable. Some critics have endeavored to prove that
there was no deer-park at Charlecote at that time; but
Lucy had other estates in the neighborhood, on some
of which he employed game-keepers, and in March,
1585, about the date of the alleged poaching, he introduced a bill into Parliament for the better preservation
of game.

The strongest argument in favor of the tradition is
to be based on the evidence furnished by the plays that
Shakespeare had a grudge against Sir Thomas, and car-
icatured him as Justice Shallow in *Henry IV.* and *The
Merry Wives of Windsor.* The reference in the latter
play to the "dozen white luces" on Shallow's coat of
arms is palpably meant to suggest the three luces, or
pikes, in the arms of the Lucys. The manner in which
the dialogue dwells on the device indicates that some
personal satire was intended.

It should be understood that poaching was then regarded, except by the victims of it, as a venial offence.
Sir Philip Sidney's May Lady calls deer-stealing "a
prettie service." The students at Oxford were the
most notorious poachers in the kingdom, in spite of laws

making expulsion from the university the penalty of de-
tection. Dr. Forman relates how two students in 1573
(one of whom afterwards became Bishop of Worcester) were more given to such pursuits than to study;
and one good man lamented in later life that he had
missed the advantages that others had derived from

ENTRANCE TO CHARLECOTE HALL

these exploits, which he believed to be an excellent
kind of discipline for young men,

We must not assume that Sir Thomas was fairly represented in the character of Justice Shallow. On the
contrary, he appears to have been an able man and
magistrate, and very genial withal. The Stratford records bear frequent testimony to his judicial services;
and his attendance on such occasions is generally

coupled with a charge for claret and sack or similar beverages. It is rather amusing that these entries occur even when he is sitting in judgment on tipplers. In the records for 1586 we read: " Paid for wine and sugar when Sir Thomas Lucy sat in commission for tipplers, xx.*d.*"

That he was a good husband we may infer from the long epitaph of his wife in Charlecote Church, which,

SIR THOMAS LUCY

after stating that she died in 1595, at the age of 63, goes on thus : "all the time of her life a true and faithful servant of her good God ; never detected of any crime or vice; in religion most sound; in love to her husband most faithful and true ; in friendship most constant; to what in trust was committed to her most secret; in wisdom excelling ; in governing of her house and bringing up of youth in the fear of God that did converse with her, most rare and singular; a great maintainer of hospitality; greatly esteemed of her betters, misliked of none unless of the envious. When all is spoken that can be said, a woman so furnished and garnished with virtue as not to be bettered, and hardly to be equalled by any. As she lived most virtuously, so she died most godly. Set down by him that best did know what hath been written to be true, *Thomas Lucy.*"

The author of this beautiful tribute may have been a severe magistrate, but he could not have been a Robert Shallow either in his official capacity or as a man.

STRATFORD-ON-AVON.

Stratford lies on a gentle slope declining to the Avon, whose banks are here shaded by venerable willows, which the poet may have had in mind when he painted the scene of poor Ophelia's death:—

> "There is a willow grows aslant a brook,
> That shows his hoar leaves in the glassy stream."

The description could have been written only by one who had observed the reflection of the white underside of the willow-leaves in the water over which they hung. And I cannot help believing that Shakespeare was mindful of the Avon when in far-away London he wrote that singularly musical simile of the river in one of his earliest plays, *The Two Gentlemen of Verona*, so aptly does it give the characteristics of the Warwick-shire stream:

> "The current that with gentle murmur glides,
> Thou know'st, being stopp'd, impatiently doth rage;
> But when his fair course is not hindered,
> He makes sweet music with the enamell'd stones,
> Giving a gentle kiss to every sedge
> He overtaketh in his pilgrimage;
> And so by many winding nooks he strays,
> With willing sport, to the wild ocean.
> Then let me go, and hinder not my course:
> I'll be as patient as a gentle stream,

And make a pastime of each weary step,
Till the last step have brought me to my love;
And there I'll rest, as, after much turmoil,
A blessed soul doth in Elysium."

The river cannot now be materially different from what it was three hundred years ago, but the town has changed a good deal. I fear that we might not have enjoyed a visit to it in that olden time as we do in these latter days.

It is not pleasant to learn that the poet's father was fined for maintaining a *sterquinarium*, which being translated from the Latin is *dung-heap*, in front of his house in Henley Street—now, like the other Stratford streets, kept as clean as any cottage-floor in the town —and we have ample evidence that the general sanitary condition of the place was very bad. John Shakespeare would probably not have been fined if his *sterquinarium* had been behind his house instead of before it.

Stratford, however, was no worse in this respect than other English towns. The terrible plagues that devastated the entire land in those " good old times" were the natural result of the unwholesome habits of life everywhere prevailing—*everywhere*, for the mansions of noblemen and the palaces of kings were as filthy as the hovels of peasants. The rushes with which royal presence-chamber and banquet-hall were strewn in place of carpets were not changed until they had become too unsavory for endurance. Meanwhile disagreeable odors were overcome by burning perfumes—of which practice we have a hint in *Much Ado About Nothing* in the reference to " smoking a musty room."

But away from these musty rooms of great men's houses, and the foul streets and lanes of towns, field and forest and river-bank were as clean and sweet as now. The banished Duke in *As You Like It* may have had other reasons than he gives for preferring life in the Forest of Arden to that of the court from which he had been driven; and Shakespeare's delight in out-of-door life may have been intensified by his experience of the house in Henley Street, with the reeking pile of filth at the front door.

His poetry is everywhere full of the beauty and fragrance of the flowers that bloom in and about Stratford; and the wonderful accuracy of his allusions to them—their colors, their habits, their time of blossoming, everything concerning them—shows how thoroughly at home he was with them, how intensely he loved and studied them.

Mr. J. R. Wise, in his *Shakespeare, His Birthplace and its Neighbourhood*, says: "Take up what play you will, and you will find glimpses of the scenery round Stratford. His maidens ever sing of 'blue-veined violets,' and 'daisies pied,' and 'pansies that are for thoughts,' and 'ladies'-smocks all silver-white,' that still stud the meadows of the Avon. . . . I do not think it is any exaggeration to say that nowhere are meadows so full of beauty as those round Stratford. I have seen them by the riverside in early spring burnished with gold; and then later, a little before hay-harvest, chased with orchises, and blue and white milkwort, and yellow rattle-grass, and tall moon-daisies : and I know nowhere woodlands so sweet as those round Stratford, filled with the soft green light made by the budding leaves, and paved with the golden ore of primroses, and their banks veined with violets. All this, and the tenderness that such beauty gives, you find in the pages of Shakespeare; and it is not too much to say that he painted them because they were ever associated in his mind with all that he held precious and dear, both of the earliest and the latest scenes of his life."

THE EARLY HISTORY OF STRATFORD.

Stratford is a very ancient town. Its name shows that it was situated at a *ford* on the Roman *street*, or highway, from London to Birmingham; but whether it was an inhabited place during the Roman occupation is uncertain. The earliest known reference to the town is in a charter dated A.D. 691, according to which Egwin, the Bishop of Worcester, obtained from Ethelred, King of Mercia, "the monastery of Stratford," with lands of about three thousand acres, in exchange for a religious house built by the bishop at Fladbury. It is not improbable that Stratford owes its foundation to this monastic settlement. Tradition says that the monastery stood where the church now is; and, as elsewhere in England, the first houses of the town were probably erected for its servants and dependants. These dwellings were doubtless near the river, in the street that has been known for centuries as "Old Town."

The district continued to be a manor of the Bishop of Worcester until after the Norman Conquest in 1066. According to the Domesday survey in 1085, its territory was "fourteen and a half hides," or about two thousand acres. It was of smaller extent than in 691, because the neighboring villages had become separate manors. The inhabitants were a priest, who doubtless

officiated in the chapel of the old monastery (of which
we find no mention after the year 872), with twenty-one
villeins and seven *bordarii*, or cottagers. The families
of these residents would make up a population of about
one hundred and fifty. "Every householder, whether
villein or cottager, evidently possessed a plough. The
community owned altogether thirty-one ploughs, of which
three belonged to the bishop, the lord of the manor."
The agricultural produce was chiefly wheat, barley, and
oats. A water-mill stood by the river, probably where
the old mill now is; and there the villagers were obliged
to grind all their corn, paying a fee for the privilege.
In 1085 the annual income from the mill was ten shillings, but the bishop was often willing to accept eels in
payment of the fees, and a thousand eels were then
sent yearly to Worcester by the people who used the
mill.

During the 12th century Stratford appears to have
made little progress. Alveston, now a small village on
the other side of the Avon, seemed likely then to rival
it in prosperity. The boundaries of the Alveston manor
were gradually extended until they reached their present limit on the south side of the bridge at Stratford
(at that time a rude wooden structure), and there a
little colony was planted which was known until after
the Elizabethan period as Bridgetown.

We get an idea of the life led by the majority of the
inhabitants of Stratford and its vicinity in the 12th and
13th centuries from the ecclesiastical records of the
various services and payments rendered as rent. Many
of the large estates outside of the town had been let as
"knight's fees," that is, on condition of certain military
services to be performed by the holders. Some of the

villeins within the village had become "free tenants," or free from serfdom, and were permitted to cultivate their land as they pleased on payment of a fixed rental in money, with little or no labor service in addition. But most of the inhabitants were still villeins or cottagers, from whom labor service was regularly exacted. "Villeins who owned sixty acres had to supply two men for reaping the lord's fields, and cottagers with thirty acres supplied one. On a special day an additional reaping service was to be performed by villeins and cottagers with all their families except their wives and shepherds. Each of the free tenants had then also to find a reaper, and to direct the reaping himself. . . . The villein was to provide two carts for the conveyance of the corn to the barns, and every cottager who owned a horse provided one cart, for the use of which he was to receive a good morning meal of bread and cheese. One day's hoeing was expected of the villein and three days' ploughing, and if an additional day were called for, food was supplied free to the workers. . . . No villein nor cottager was allowed to bring up his child for the church without permission of the lord of the manor. A fee had to be paid when a daughter of a villein or cottager was married. On his death his best wagon was claimed by the steward in his lord's behalf, and a fine of money was exacted from his successor— if, as the record wisely adds, he could pay one. Any townsman who made beer for sale paid for the privilege."

In 1197 the inhabitants obtained for the town from Richard I. the privilege of a weekly market, to be holden on Thursdays, for which the citizens paid the bishop a yearly toll of sixteen shillings. The market was doubtless held at first in the open space still known as the Rother Market, in the centre of which the Memorial Fountain, the gift of Mr. George W. Childs of Philadelphia, now stands. *Rother* is an old word, of Anglo-Saxon origin, applied to cattle, which must have been a staple commodity in the early Stratford market. The term was familiar to Shakespeare, who uses it in *Timon of Athens* (iv. 3. 12) :—

> " It is the pasture lards the rother's sides,
>   The want that makes him lean."

In the course of the 11th century Stratford was also endowed with a series of annual fairs, " the chief stimulants of trade in the middle ages." The earliest of these fairs was granted by the Bishop of Worcester in 1216, to begin " on the eve of the Holy Trinity, and to continue for the next two days ensuing." In 1224 a fair was established for the eve of St. Augustine (May 26th) " and on the day and morrow after "; in 1242, for the eve of the Exaltation of the Holy Cross (September 14th), " the day, and two days following "; and in 1271, " for the eve of the Ascension of our Lord, commonly called Holy Thursday, and upon the day and morrow following." Early in the next century (1313) another fair was instituted, to begin on the eve of St. Peter and St. Paul (June 29th) and to be held for fifteen days.

Trinity Sunday was doubtless chosen for the opening of the first of these fairs because the parish church was dedicated to the Holy Trinity, and a festival in commemoration of the dedication of the church was celebrated on that Sunday by a " wake," which attracted

STRATFORD CHURCH

many people from the neighboring villages. "There was nothing exceptional in a Sunday of specially sacred character being turned to commercial uses. In most medieval towns, moreover, traders exposed their wares at fair-time in the churchyard, and chaffering and bargaining were conducted in the church itself." Attempts were made by the ecclesiastical authorities to restrain these practices, but they continued until the Reformation.

At the close of the 13th century the prosperity of Stratford was assured. Alveston had then ceased to be a dangerous rival. The town was more and more profitable to the Bishops of Worcester, who interested themselves in promoting its welfare. It appears also that Bishop Gifford had a park here ; for on the 3d of May, 1280, he sent his injunctions to the deans of Stratford and the adjacent towns "solemnly to excommunicate all those that had broke his park and stole his deer."

In the 14th century the condition of the Stratford folk materially improved. Villeinage gradually disappeared in the reign of Edward III. (1327-1377), and those who had been subject to it became free tenants, paying definite rents for house and land. Three natives of the town, who, after the fashion of the time, took their surnames from the place of their birth, rose to high positions in the Church, one becoming Archbishop of Canterbury, and the others respectively Bishops of London and Chichester. John of Stratford and Robert of Stratford were brothers, and Ralph of Stratford was their nephew. John and Robert were both for a time Chancellors of England, and there is no other instance of two brothers attaining that high office in succession.

All three had a great affection for their native town, and did much to promote its welfare. Robert, while holding the living of Stratford, took measures for the

STRATFORD CHURCH, WEST END

paving of some of the main streets. John enlarged the parish church, rebuilding portions of it, and founded a chantry with five priests to perform masses for the souls of the founder and his friends. Later he purchased the patronage of Stratford from the Bishop of Worcester, and gave it to his chantry priests, who thus came into full control of the parish church. Ralph, in 1351, built for the chantry priests "a house of square stone for the habitation of these priests, adjoining to the churchyard." This building, afterwards known as the College, remained in possession of the priests until 1546, when Henry VIII. included it in the dissolution of monastic establishments. After passing through various hands as a private residence, it was finally taken down in 1799.

Other inhabitants of Stratford followed the example set by John and Ralph in their benefactions to the church. Dr. Thomas Bursall, warden of the College in the time of Edward IV., added "a fair and beautiful choir, rebuilt from the ground at his own cost"—the choir which is still the most beautiful portion of the venerable edifice, and in which Shakespeare lies buried.

The only important alteration in the church since Shakespeare's day was the erection of the present spire in 1764, to replace a wooden one covered with lead and about forty feet high, which had been taken down a year before. The tower is the oldest part of the church as it now exists, and was probably built before the year 1200. It is eighty feet high, to which the spire adds eighty-three feet more.

The last of the early benefactors of Stratford was Sir Hugh Clopton, who came from the neighboring village of Clopton about 1480. A few years later he built "a pretty house of brick and timber wherein he lived in his latter days." This was the mansion afterwards known as New Place, which in 1597 became the property of William Shakespeare, and was his residence

3

after he returned to his native town about 1611 or
1612.

Sir Hugh also built "the great bridge upon the Avon,
at the east end of the town," constructed of freestone,
with fourteen arches, and a "long causeway" of stone,
"well walled on each side." . . . Before this time, as
Leland the antiquarian wrote about 1530, "there was
but a poor bridge of timber, and no causeway to come
to it, whereby many poor folk either refused to come to
Stratford when the river was up, or coming thither
stood in jeopardy of life." This bridge, though often
repaired, is to this day a monument to Sir Hugh's public spirit.

THE STRATFORD GUILD.

In the latter part of the 13th century an institution
attained a position and influence in Stratford which
were destined to deprive the Bishops of Worcester of
their authority in the government of the town. This
was the Guild of the Holy Cross, the Blessed Virgin,
and St. John the Baptist, as it was then called. The
triple name has suggested that it was formed by the
union of three separate guilds, but of this no historical
evidence has been discovered.

This guild, like other of these ancient societies, had
a religious origin, being "collected for the love of God
and our souls' need"; but relief of the poor and of its
own indigent members was also a part of its functions.

The "craft-guilds," formed by people engaged in a
single trade or occupation, were a different class of societies, though in many instances offshoots from the religious guilds, and often, as in London, surviving the
decay of the parent institution.

Members of both sexes were admitted to the Stratford Guild, as to others of its class, on payment of a small annual fee. "This primarily secured for them

THE GUILD CHAPEL AND GRAMMAR SCHOOL, STRATFORD

the performance of certain religious rites, which were more valued than life itself. While the members lived, but more especially after their death, lighted tapers were duly distributed in their behalf, before the altars of

the Virgin and of their patron saints in the parish
church. A poor man in the Middle Ages found it very
difficult, without the intervention of the guilds, to keep
this road to salvation always open. Gifts were frequently awarded to members anxious to make pilgrim-
ages to Canterbury, and at times the spinster members
received dowries from the association. The regulation
which compelled the members to attend the funeral of
any of their fellows united them among themselves in
close bonds of intimacy."

The social spirit was fostered yet more by a great
annual meeting, at which all members were expected
to be present in special uniform. They marched with
banners flying in procession to church, and afterwards
sat down together to a generous feast.

Though of religious origin the guilds were strictly
lay associations. In many towns priests were excluded
from membership; if admitted, they had no more authority or influence than laymen. Priests were employed to perform the religious services of the guild,
for which they were duly paid; but the fraternities were
governed by their own elected officers—wardens, aldermen, beadles, and clerks—and a council of their representatives controlled their property and looked after
their rights.

When the Stratford Guild was founded it is impossible to determine. "Its beginning," as its chief officers wrote in 1389, "was from time whereunto the memory of man reacheth not." Records preserved in the
town prove that it was in existence early in the 13th
century, and that bequests were then made to it. The
Bishops of Worcester encouraged such gifts, and apparently managed that some of the revenues of the Guild

should be devoted to ecclesiastical purposes outside
its own regular uses. Before the time of Edward I.
the society was rich in houses and lands; and in 1353,
as its records show, it owned a house in almost every
street in Stratford.

In 1296 the elder Robert of Stratford, father of John
and Robert (p. 31), laid the foundation of a special
chapel for the Guild, and also of adjacent almshouses.
These doubtless stood where the present chapel, Guildhall, and other fraternfty buildings now are.

In 1332 Edward III. gave the Guild a charter con-
firming its right to all its property and to the full control
of its own affairs. In 1389 Richard II. sent out commissioners to report upon the ordinances of the guilds
throughout England, and the report for Stratford is still
extant. It shows what a good work the society was
doing for the relief of the poor and for the promotion
of fraternal relations among its members. Regulations
for the government of the Guild by two wardens or
aldermen and six others indicate the progress of the
town in the direction of self-government. An association which had come to include all the substantial house-
holders naturally acquired much jurisdiction in civil
affairs. Its members referred their disputes with one
another to its council; and the aldermen gradually became the administrators of the municipal police. The
College priests were very jealous of the Guild's increasing influence, and when the society resisted the payment of tithes they brought a lawsuit to compel the
fulfilment of this ancient obligation; but in all other
respects the Guild appears to have been independent
of external control.

A curious feature of the conditions of membership in

the 15th century was that the souls of the dead could be admitted to its spiritual privileges on payment of the regular fees by the living. Early in the century six dead children of John Whittington of Stratford were allowed this benefit for the sum of ten shillings.

The fame of the institution in its palmy days spread far beyond the limits of Stratford, and attracted not a few men of the highest rank and reputation. George, Duke of Clarence, brother of Edward IV., and his wife, were enrolled among its members, with Edward Lord Warwick and Margaret, two of their children; and the distinguished judge, Sir Thomas Lyttleton, received the same honor. Few towns or villages of Warwickshire were without representation in it, and merchants joined it from places as far away as Bristol and Peterborough.

To us, however, the most remarkable fact in the history of the Guild is the establishment of the Grammar School for the children of its members. The date of its foundation has been usually given as 1453, but it is now known to have been in existence before that time. Attendance was free, and the master, who was paid ten pounds a year by the Guild, was forbidden to take anything from the pupils. In this school, as we shall see later, William Shakespeare was educated, and we shall become better acquainted with it when we follow the boy thither.

The Guild Chapel, with the exception of the chancel, which had been renovated about 1450, was taken down and rebuilt in the closing years of the century by Sir Hugh Clopton (see page 34 above), who was a prominent member of the fraternity. The work was not finished until after his death in September, 1496, but the expense of its completion was provided for in his will.

THE STRATFORD CORPORATION.

The Guild was dissolved by Henry VIII. in 1547, and its possessions remained as crown property until 1553. For seven years the town had been without any responsible government. Meanwhile the leading citizens — the old officers of the Guild — had petitioned Edward VI. to restore that society as a municipal corporation. He granted their prayer, and by a charter dated June 7, 1553, put the government of the town in the hands of its inhabitants. The estates, revenues, and chattels of the Guild were made over to the corporation, which, as the heir and successor of the venerable fraternity, adopted the main features of its organization. The names and functions of its chief officers were but slightly changed. The warden became the bailiff, and the proctors were called chamberlains, but aldermen, clerk, and beadle resumed their old titles. The common council continued to meet monthly in the Guildhall; but it now included, besides the bailiff and ten aldermen, the ten chief burgesses, and its authority covered the whole town. The fraternal sentiment of the ancient society survived; it being ordered "that none of the aldermen nor none of the capital burgesses, neither in the council chamber nor elsewhere, do revile one another, but brother-like live together, and that after they be entered into the council chamber, that they nor none of them depart not forth but in brotherly love, under the pains of every offender to forfeit and pay for every default, vj*s*. viij*d*." When any councillor or his wife died, all were to attend the funeral "in their honest apparel, and bring the corpse to the church, there to continue and abide devoutly until the corpse be buried."

The Grammar School and the chapel and almshouses of the Guild became public institutions. The bailiff became a magistrate who presided at a monthly court for the recovery of small debts, and at the higher semi-annual *leets*, or court-leets, to which all the inhabitants were summoned to revise and enforce the police regulations. Shakespeare alludes to these leets in *The Taming of the Shrew* (ind. 2. 89) where the servant tells Kit Sly that he has been talking in his sleep:—

" Yet would you say ye were beaten out of door,
　And rail upon the mistress of the house,
　And say you would present her at the leet
　Because she brought stone jugs and no seal'd quarts."

And Iago (*Othello*, iii. 3. 140) refers to " leets and law-days." Prices of bread and beer were fixed by the council, and ale-tasters were annually appointed to see that the orders concerning the quality and price of malt liquors and bread were enforced. Shakespeare's father was an ale-taster in 1557, and about the same time was received into the corporation as a burgess. In 1561 he was elected as one of the two chamberlains ; in 1565 he became an alderman ; and in 1568 he was chosen bailiff, the highest official position in the town.

The rule of the council was of a very paternal character. " If a man lived immorally he was summoned to the Guildhall, and rigorously examined as to the truth of the rumors that had reached the bailiff's ear. If his guilt was proved, and he refused to make adequate reparation, he was invited to leave the town. Rude endeavors were made to sweeten the tempers of scolding wives. A substantial 'ducking-stool,' with iron staples, lock, and hinges, was kept in good repair. The shrew was attached to it, and by means of ropes, planks, and wheels was plunged two or three times into the Avon whenever the municipal council believed her to stand in need of correction. Three days and three nights were invariably spent in the open stocks by any inhabitant who spoke disrespectfully to any town officer, or who disobeyed any minor municipal decree. No one might receive a stranger into his house without the bailiff's permission. No journeyman, apprentice, or servant might 'be forth of their or his master's house' after nine o'clock at night. Bowling-alleys and butts were provided by the council, but were only to be used at stated times. An alderman was fined on one occasion for going to bowls after a morning meeting of the council, and Henry Sydnall was fined twenty pence for keeping unlawful or unlicensed bowling in a back shed. Alehouse-keepers, of whom there were thirty in Shakespeare's time, were kept strictly under the council's control. They were not allowed to brew their own ale, or to encourage tippling, or to serve poor artificers except at stated hours of the day, on pain of fine and imprisonment. Dogs were not to go about the streets unmuzzled. Every inhabitant had to go to church at least once a month, and absences were liable to penalties of twenty pounds, which in the late years of Elizabeth's reign commissioners came from London to see that the local authorities enforced. Early in the 17th century swearing was rigorously prohibited. Laws as to dress were regularly enforced. In 1577 there were many fines exacted for failure to wear the plain statute woollen caps on Sundays, to which Rosaline makes allusion in *Love's Labour's Lost* (v. 2. 281); and the regulation

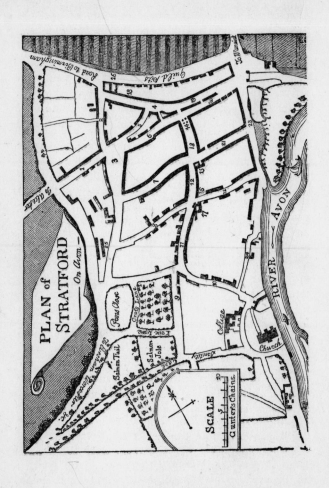

PLAN of
STRATFORD
— On Avon —

Road to Birmingham

Guild Field

To Warwick

To Alcester

RIVER — AVON

Pond Close

Cross Lane

Love Lane

Salmon Tail

Salmon Jole

College

Church

Chapel

SCALE

Gunters Chains.

affected all inhabitants above six years of age. In 1604 'the greatest part' of the inhabitants were presented at a great leet, or law-day, 'for wearing their apparel contrary to the statute.' Nor would it be difficult to quote many other like proofs of the persistent strictness with which the new town council of Stratford, by the enforcement of its own order and the statutes of the realm, regulated the inhabitants' whole conduct of life."

THE TOPOGRAPHY OF STRATFORD.

No map of Stratford made before the middle of the 18th century is known to exist. The one here given in fac-simile was executed about the year 1768, and, as Mr. Halliwell-Phillipps tells us, "it clearly appears from the local records that there had then been no material alteration in either the form or the extent of the town since the days of Elizabeth. It may therefore be accepted as a reliable guide to the locality as it existed in the poet's own time, when the number of inhabited houses, exclusive of mere hovels, could not have much exceeded five hundred."

The following is a copy of the references which are appended to the original map: " 1. Moor Town's End; —2. Henley Lane; — 3. Rother Market; —4. Henley Street; — 5. Meer Pool Lane; —6. Wood Street; —7. Ely Street or Swine Street; —8. Scholar's Lane alias Tinker's Lane; —9. Bull Lane; —10. Street call'd Old Town; —11. Church Street; —12. Chapel Street; —13. High Street; —14. Market Cross; —15. Town Hall; — 16. Place where died Shakespeare; —17. Chapel, Public Schools, &c.; — 18. House where was Shakespeare born; — 19. Back Bridge Street; — 20. Fore Bridge

Street;—21. Sheep Street;—22. Chapel Lane;—23. Buildings call'd Water Side;—24. Southam's Lane;—25. Dissenting Meeting;—26. White Lion."

Moor Town's End (1) is now Greenhill Street. The Town Hall (15) did not exist in Shakespeare's time, having been first erected in 1633, taken down in 1767, and rebuilt the following year. The "Place where died Shakespeare" (16) was New Place, the home of his later years. The "Dissenting Meeting" or Meeting-house (25) was built long after the poet's day. The "White Lion" (26) was also post-Shakespearian, the chief inns in the 16th century being the Swan, the Bear, and the Crown, all in Bridge Street. The Mill and Mill Bridge (built in 1590) are indicated on the river at the left-hand lower corner of the map; and the stone bridge, erected by Sir Hugh Clopton about 1500, is just outside the right-hand lower corner.

The only important change in the streets since the map was made is the removal of the row of small shops and stalls, known as Middle Row, between Fore Bridge Street (20); and Back Bridge Street (19); thus making the broad avenue now called Bridge Street.

The "Market Cross" (14) was "a stone monument covered by a low tiled shed, round which were benches for the accommodation of listeners to the sermons which, as at St. Paul's Cross in London, were some-times preached there." Later a room was added above, and a clock above that. The open space about the Cross was the chief market-place of the town. Near by was a pump, at which housewives were frequently to be seen "washing of clothes" and hanging them on the cross to dry, and butchers sometimes hung meat there; but these practices were forbidden by the town council in 1608. The stocks, pillory, and whipping-post were in the same locality.

There was also a stone cross in the Rother Market (3), and near the Guild Chapel (17) was a second pump, which was removed by order of the council in 1595. The field on the river, near the foot of Chapel Lane (22), was known as the Bank-croft, or Bancroft, where drovers and farmers of the town were allowed to take their cattle to pasture for an hour daily. "All horses, geldings, mares, swine, geese, ducks, and other cattle," according to the regulation established by the council, if found there in violation of this restriction, were put by the beadle into the "pinfold," or pound, which was not far off. This Bancroft, as it is still called, is now part of the beautiful little park on the river-bank, adjacent to the grounds of the Shakespeare Memorial.

Chapel Lane, which bounded one side of the New Place estate, was one of the filthiest thoroughfares of the town, the general sanitary condition of which (see page 25 above) was bad enough. A streamlet ran through it, the water of which turned a mill, alluded to in town records of that period. This water-course gradually became "a shallow fetid ditch, an open receptacle of sewage and filth." It continued to be a nuisance for at least two centuries more. A letter written in 1807, in connection with a lawsuit, gives some interesting reminiscences of it. "I very well remember," says the writer, "the ditch you mention forty-five years, as after my sister was married, which was in October, 1760, I was very often at Stratford, and was very well acquainted both with the ditch and the road in question; — the ditch went from the Chapel, and extended to Smith's house; — I well remember there was a space of two or three feet from the wall in a descent to the ditch, and I do not think any part of the new wall was built on the ditch;—the ditch was the receptacle for all manner of filth that any person chose to put there, and was very obnoxious at times;—Mr. Hunt used to complain of it, and was determined to get it covered over, or he would do it at his own expense, and I do not know whether he did or not;—across, the road from the ditch to Shakespeare Garden was very hollow and always full of mud, which is now covered over, and in general there was only one wagon tract along the lane, which used to be very bad, in the winter particularly;—I do not know that the ditch was so deep as to overturn a carriage, and the road was very little used near it, unless it was to turn out for another, as there was always room enough." Thomas Cox, a carpenter, who lived in Chapel Lane from 1774, remembered that the open gutter from the Chapel to Smith's cottage "was a wide dirty ditch choked with mud, that all the filth of that part of the town ran into it, that it was four or five feet wide and more than a foot deep, and that the road sloped down to the ditch." According to other witnesses, the ditch extended to the end of the lane, where, between the roadway and the Bancroft, was a narrow creek or ditch through which the overflow from Chapel Lane no doubt found a way into the river.

Mr. Halliwell-Phillipps believes that the fever which proved fatal to Shakespeare was caused by the "wretched sanitary conditions surrounding his residence"—an explanation of it which would never have occurred even to medical men in that day.

Part II
HIS HOME LIFE

ROOM IN WHICH SHAKESPEARE WAS BORN

SHAKESPEARE HOUSE, RESTORED

THE DWELLING-HOUSES OF THE TIME

THE house in Henley Street in which William Shakespeare was probably born and spent his early years has
undergone many changes; but, as carefully restored
in recent years and reverently preserved for a national
memorial of the poet, its appearance now is doubtless
not materially different from what it was in the latter
part of the 16th century.

There are a few houses of the same period and the
same class still standing in Stratford and its vicinity,

which, according to the highest antiquarian authority,
are almost unaltered from their original form and finish.
Mr. Halliwell-Phillipps mentions one in particular in
the Rother Market, "the main features of which are
certainly in their original state," and the sketches of
the interior given by him closely resemble those of the
Shakespeare house.

These houses were usually of two stories, and were
constructed of wooden beams, forming a framework,
the spaces between the beams being filled with lath
and plaster. The roofs were usually of thatch, with
dormer windows and steep gables. The door was
shaded by a porch or by a *pentice*, or *penthouse*, which
was a narrow sloping roof often extending along the
the front of the lower story over both door and windows, as in Shakespeare's birthplace on Henley Street.

In the *Merchant of Venice* (ii. 6. 1) Gratiano says:—

> "This is the penthouse under which Lorenzo
>   Desired us to make stand."

In *Much Ado About Nothing* (iii. 3. 110) Borachio
says to Conrade: "Stand thee close, then, under this
penthouse, for it drizzles rain." We find a figurative
allusion to the penthouse in *Love's Labour 's Lost* (iii.
1. 17): "with your hat penthouse-like o'er the shop
of your eyes"; and another in *Macbeth* (i. 3. 20):—

> "Sleep shall neither night nor day
>   Hang upon his penthouse lid";

the projecting eyebrow being compared to this part of
the Elizabethan dwelling.

The better houses, like New Place, were of timber and brick, instead of plaster, though sometimes entirely of stone. Shakespeare appears to have rebuilt the greater part of New Place with stone. The roofs of this class of dwellings were usually tiled, but occasionally thatched. We read of one Walter Roche, who in 1582 replaced the tiles of his house in Chapel Street with thatch. The wood-work in the front of some houses, as in a fine example still to be seen in the High Street (page 59 below), was elaborately carved with floral and other designs.

The gardens were bounded by walls constructed of clay or mud and usually thatched at the top. Fruit-trees were common in these gardens, and the orchard about the Guild buildings was noted for its plums and apples. When the mulberry-tree was first introduced into England, Shakespeare bought one and set it out in his grounds at New Place, where it grew to great size. It survived for nearly a century and a half after the death of the poet, but in 1758 was cut down by the Rev. Francis Gastrell, who had bought the estate in 1756.

There was little of what we should regard as comfort in those picturesque old English houses, with their great black beams chequering the outer walls into squares and triangles, their small many-paned windows, their low ceilings and rude interior wood-work, their poor and scanty furnishings.

Chimneys had but just come into general use in England, and, though John Shakespeare's house had one, the dwellings of many of his neighbors were still unprovided with them. In 1582, when William was eighteen years old, an order was passed by the town council that "Walter Hill, dwelling in Rother Market, and all the other inhabitants of the borough, shall, before St. James's Day, 30th April, make sufficient chimneys," under pain of a fine of ten shillings.

This was intended as a precaution against fires, the frequent occurrence of which in former years had been mainly due to the absence of chimneys.

William Harrison, in 1577, referring to things in England that had been "marvellously changed within the memory of old people," includes among these "the multitude of chimneys lately erected, whereas in their young days there were not above two or three, if so many, in most uplandish towns of the realm (the religious houses and manor places of their lords always excepted), but each one made his fire against a reredos* in the hall, where he dined and dressed his meat.

In another chapter Harrison says : "Now have we many chimneys ; and yet our tenderlings complain of rheums, catarrhs, and poses. Then had we none but reredosses ; and our heads did never ache. For as the smoke in those days was supposed to be a sufficient hardening for the timber of the house, so it was reported a far better medicine to keep the goodman and his family from the quack or pose, wherewith, as then, very few were acquainted."

THE HOUSEHOLD FURNITURE.

Of the furniture in these old houses we get an idea from inventories of the period that have come down to

---

* A *reredos* was a kind of open hearth or brazier. *Pose*, just below, means a cold in the head, and *quack* a hoarseness or croaking caused by a cold in the throat.

us. We have, for instance, such a list of the house-hold equipment of Richard Arden, Shakespeare's ma-ternal grandfather, who was a wealthy farmer; and another of such property belonging to Henry Field, tanner, a neighbor of John Shakespeare, who was his chief executor.

From these and similar inventories we find that the only furniture in the hall, or main room of the house—often occupying the whole of the ground floor—and the parlor, or sitting-room, when there was one, consisted of two or three chairs, a few joint-stools—that is, stools made of wood jointed or fitted together, as distinguished from those more rudely made—a table of the plainest construction, and possibly one or more "painted cloths" hung on the walls.

These painted cloths were cheap substitutes for the tapestries with which great mansions were adorned, and they were often found in the cottages of the poor. The paintings were generally crude representations of Biblical stories, together with maxims or mottoes, which were sometimes on scrolls or "labels" proceeding from the mouths of the characters.

Shakespeare refers to these cloths several times; for instance, in *As You Like It* (iii. 2. 291), where Jaques says to Orlando : "You are full of pretty answers ; have you not been acquainted with goldsmiths' wives and conned them out of rings?"—referring to the mottoes, or "posies," as they were called, often inscribed in finger-rings. Orlando replies : "Not so; but I answer you right painted cloth, from whence you have studied your questions." Falstaff (1 *Henry IV.* iv. 2. 28) says that his recruits are "ragged as Lazarus in the painted cloth."

In an anonymous play, *No Whipping nor Tripping*, printed in 1601, we find this passage :—

> "Read what is written on the painted cloth :
> Do no man wrong ; be good unto the poor ;
> Beware the mouse, the maggot, and the moth,
> And ever have an eye unto the door," etc.

When carpets are mentioned in these inventories, they are coverings for the tables, not for the floors, which, even in kings' palaces, were strewn with rushes. Grumio, in *The Taming of the Shrew* (iv. 1. 52) sees "the carpets laid" for supper on his master's return home. A Stratford inventory of 1590 mentions "a carpet for a table." Carpets were also used for window-seats, but were seldom placed on the floor except to kneel upon, or for other special purposes. .

The bedroom furniture was equally rude and scanty, though better than it had been when the old folk of the time were young. Harrison says :—

"Our fathers and we ourselves have lien full oft upon straw pallets covered only with a sheet, under coverlets made of dagswain or hopharlots [coarse, rough cloths], and a good round log under their heads instead of a bolster. If it were that our fathers or the good man of the house had a mattress or flock-bed, and thereto a sack of chaff to rest his head upon, he thought himself to be as well lodged as the lord of the town, so well were they contented."

But feather beds had now come into use, with pillows, and "flaxen sheets," and other comfortable appliances. Henry Field had "one bed-covering of yellow and green" among his household goods.

Kitchen utensils and table-ware had likewise improved within the memory of the old inhabitant, though still rude and simple enough. Harrison notes "the exchange of treen [wooden] platters into pewter, and wooden spoons into silver or tin."

He adds: "So common were all sorts of treen stuff in old time that a man should hardly find four pieces of pewter (of which one was peradventure a salt) in a good farmer's house"; but now they had plenty of pewter, with perhaps a silver bowl and salt-cellar, and a dozen silver spoons.

The table-linen was hempen for common use, but flaxen for special occasions, and the napkins were of the same materials. These napkins, or towels, as they were sometimes called, were for wiping the hands after eating with the fingers, forks being as yet unknown in England except as a curiosity.

Elizabeth is the first royal personage in the country who is known to have had a fork, and it is doubtful whether she used it. It was not until the middle of the 17th century that forks were used even by the higher classes, and silver forks were not introduced until about 1814.

Thomas Coryat, in his *Crudities*, published in 1611, only five years before Shakespeare died, gives an account of the use of forks in Italy, where they appear to have been invented in the 15th century. He says:—

"The Italian and also most strangers do always at their meals use a little fork when they do cut their meat. For while with their knife, which they hold in one hand, they cut the meat out of the dish, they fasten the fork, which they hold in their other hand, upon the same dish; so that whosoever he be that, sitting in the company of others at meals, should unadvisedly touch the dish of meat with his fingers, from which all the table do cut, he will give occasion of offence unto the company, as having transgressed the laws of good manners."

Coryat adds that he himself "thought good to imitate the Italian fashion by this forked cutting of meat," not only while he was in Italy, but after he came home to England, where, however, he was sometimes "quipped" for what his friends regarded as a foreign affectation.

The dramatists of the time also refer contemptuously to "your fork-carving traveller"; and one clergyman preached against the use of forks "as being an insult to Providence not to touch one's meat with one's fingers!"

Towels, except for table use, are rarely noticed in inventories of the period, and when mentioned are specified as "washing towels." Neither are wash-basins often referred to, except in lists of articles used by barbers.

Bullein, in his *Government of Health*, published about 1558, says: "Plain people in the country use seldom times to wash their hands, as appeareth by their filthiness, and as very few times comb their heads."

Their betters were none too particular in these matters, and in personal cleanliness generally. Baths are seldom referred to in writings of the time, except for the treatment of certain diseases.

Reference has already been made to the use of rushes for covering floors. It was thought to be a piece of unnecessary luxury on the part of Wolsey when he caused the rushes at Hampton Court to be changed every day.

INTERIOR OF ANNE HATHAWAY'S COTTAGE

From a letter of Erasmus to Dr. Francis, Wolsey's physician, it would appear that the lowest layer of rushes — the top only being renewed — was sometimes unchanged for years — the latter says "twenty years," which seems hardly credible — becoming a receptacle for beer, grease, fragments of victuals, and other organic matters.

Perfumes were used for neutralizing the foul odors that resulted from this filthiness. Burton, in his *Anatomy of Melancholy*, 1621, says: "The smoke of juniper is in great request with us at Oxford, to sweeten our chambers." [See also page 25 above.]

From the correspondence of the Earl of Shrewsbury with Lord Burleigh, during the confinement of Mary Queen of Scots at Sheffield Castle, in 1572, we learn that she was to be removed for five or six days "to cleanse her chamber, being kept very uncleanly."

In a memoir written by Anne, Countess of Dorset, in 1603, we read: "We all went to Tibbals to see the King, who used my mother and my aunt very graciously; but we all saw a great change between the fashion of the Court as it was now and of that in the Queen's, for we were all lousy by sitting in Sir Thomas Erskine's chambers."

FOOD AND DRINK.

The food of the common people was better in some respects than it is nowadays, and better than it was in Continental countries. Harrison says that whereas what he calls "white meats"—milk, butter, and cheese—were in old times the food of the upper classes, they were in his time "only eaten by the poor," while all other classes ate flesh, fish, and "wild and tame fowls."

Wheaten bread, however, was little known except to the rich, the bread of the poor being made of rye or barley, and, in times of scarcity, of beans, oats, and even acorns.

Tea and coffee had not yet been introduced into England, but wine was abundant and cheap. It is rather surprising to learn that from twenty to thirty thousand tuns of home-grown wine were then made in the country.

Of foreign wines, thirty kinds of strong and fifty-six of light were to be had in London. The price ranged from eightpence to a shilling a gallon. The drink of the common people, however, was beer, which was generally home-brewed and cheap withal.

Harrison, who was a country clergyman with forty pounds a year, tells how his good wife brewed two hundred gallons at a cost of twenty shillings, or less than three halfpence a gallon. When nobody drank water, and the only substitute for malt liquors was milk, the consumption of beer was of course enormous.

The meals were but two a day. Harrison says: "Heretofore there hath been much more time spent in eating and drinking than commonly is in these days, for whereas of old we had breakfasts in the forenoon, beverages or nuntions [luncheons] after dinner, and thereto rear-suppers [late or second suppers] generally when it was time to go to rest, now these odd repasts—thanked be God—are very well left, and each one in manner (except here and there some young hungry stomach that cannot fast till dinner time) contenteth himself with dinner and supper only."

Of the times of meals he says: "With us the nobility, gentry, and students do ordinarily go to dinner at eleven

OLD HOUSE IN HIGH STREET

before noon, and to supper at five, or between five and six at afternoon. The merchants dine and sup seldom before twelve at noon and six at night, especially in London. The husbandmen dine also at high noon, as they call it, and sup at seven or eight; but out of the term in our universities the scholars dine at ten. As for the poorest sort, they generally dine and sup when they may, so that to talk of their order of repast it were but needless matter."

Rising at four or five in the morning, as was the custom with the common people, and going until ten or even noon without food must have been hard for other than the "young hungry stomachs" of which Harrison speaks so contemptuously.

THE TRAINING OF CHILDREN.

In the 16th century, children of the middle and upper classes were strictly brought up. The "Books of Nurture," published at that time, give minute directions for the behavior of boys like William at home, at school, at church, and elsewhere. These manuals were generally in doggerel verse, and several of them have been edited by Dr. F. J. Furnivall for the Early English Text Society.

Among them is one by Francis Seager, published in London in 1557, entitled *The Schoole of Vertue, and booke of good Nourture for Chyldren and youth to learne their dutie by.* Another is *The Boke of Nurture, or Schoole of good maners for men, servants, and children,* compiled by Hugh Rhodes, of which at least five editions were printed between 1554 and 1577.

The *Schoole of Vertue* begins thus * (the spelling being modernized):—

---

* In the original each of these lines is divided into two, thus:
"First in the mornynge
    when thou dost awake
To God for his grace
    thy peticion then make;" etc.
To save space, I arrange the lines as Dr. Furnivall does.

"First in the morning when thou dost awake
To God for his grace thy petition then make;
This prayer following use daily to say,
Thy heart lifting up; thus begin to pray;"

A prayer of eighteen lines follows, with directions to
repeat the Lord's Prayer after it. Then come rules
"how to order thyself when thou risest, and in apparel-
ling thy body."

The child is to rise early, dress carefully, washing
his hands and combing his head. When he goes down
stairs he is to salute the family :—

"Down from thy chamber when thou shalt go,
Thy parents salute thou, and the family also."

Elsewhere, politeness out of doors is enjoined :—

"Be free of cap [taking it off to his elders] and full of
courtesy."

At meals his first duty is to wait upon his parents,
after saying this grace :—

"Give thanks to God with one accord
For that shall be set on this board.
And be not careful what to eat,
To each thing living the Lord sends meat;
For food He will not see you perish,
But will you feed, foster, and cherish;
Take well in worth what He hath sent,
At this time be therewith content,
Praising God."

He is then to make low curtsy, saying "Much good
may it do you!" and, if he is big enough, he is to
bring the food to the table.

In filling the dishes he must take care not to get them so full as to spill anything on his parents' clothes. He is to have spare trenchers and napkins ready for guests, to see that all are supplied with "bread and drink," and that the "voiders"—the baskets or vessels into which bones are thrown—are often emptied.

When the course of meat is over he is to clear the table, cover the salt, put the dirty trenchers and napkins into a voider, sweep the crumbs into another, place a clean trencher before each person, and set on "cheese with fruit, with biscuits or caraways" [comfits containing caraway seeds, which were considered favorable to digestion, and, according to a writer on health, in 1595, "surely very good for students"], also wine, "if any there were," or beer.

The meal ended, he is to remove the cloth, turning in each side and folding it up carefully; "a clean towel then on the table to spread," and bring basin and ewer for washing the hands. He now clears the table again, and when the company rise, he must not "forget his duty":—

"Before the table make thou low curtsy."

The boy can now eat his own dinner, and equally minute directions are given as to his behavior while doing it. He is not to break his bread, but "cut it fair," not to fill his spoon too full of soup, nor his mouth too full of meat—

"Not smacking thy lips as commonly do hogs,
 Nor gnawing the bones as it were dogs.
 Such rudeness abhor, such beastliness fly,
 At the table behave thyself mannerly."

He must keep his fingers clean with a napkin, wipe his mouth before drinking, and be temperate in eating—" For 'measure is treasure,' the proverb doth say."

The directions " how to behave thyself in talking with any man " are very minute and specific:—

"If a man demand a question of thee,
In thine answer-making be not too hasty;
Weigh well his words, the case understand,
Ere an answer to make thou take in hand;
Else may he judge in thee little wit,
To answer to a thing and not hear it.
Suffer his tale whole out to be told,
Then speak thou mayst, and not be controlled;
Low obeisance making, looking him in the face,
Treatably speaking, thy words see thou place,
With countenance sober, thy body upright,
Thy feet just together, thy hands in like plight;
Cast not thine eyes on either side.
When thou art praised, therein take no pride.
In telling thy tale, neither laugh nor smile;
Such folly forsake thou, banish and exile.
In audible voice thy words do thou utter,
Not high nor low, but using a measure.
Thy words see that thou pronounce plaine,
And that they spoken be not in vain ;
In uttering whereof keep thou an order,
Thy matter thereby thou shalt much forder [further]
Which order if thou do not observe,
From the purpose needs must thou swerve,
And hastiness of speed will cause thee to err,
Or will thee teach to stut or stammer.
To stut or stammer is a foul crime;
Learn then to leave it, take warning in time,
How evil a child it doth become,
Thyself being judge, having wisdom;

And sure it is taken by custom and ure [use],
While young you be there is help and cure.
This general rule yet take with thee,
In speaking to any man thy head uncovered be,
The common proverb remember ye ought,
'Better unfed than untaught.'"

Though this may be very poor poetry, it is very good
advice; and so is this which follows, on "how to order
thyself being sent of message":—

"If of message forth thou be sent,
Take heed to the same, give ear diligent;
Depart not away and being in doubt,
Know well thy message before thou pass out;
With possible speed then haste thee right soon,
If need shall require it so to be done.
After humble obeisance the message forth shew,
Thy words well placing, in uttering but few
As shall thy matter serve to declare.
Thine answer made, then home again repair,
And to thy master thereof make relation
As then the answer shall give thee occasion.
Neither add nor diminish anything to the same,
Lest after it prove to thy rebuke and shame,
But the same utter as near as thou can;
No fault they shall find to charge thee with than
    [then]."

Similar counsel is added "against the horrible vice of
swearing":

"In vain take not the name of God;
Swear not at all for fear of his rod.
      *   *   *   *   *   *

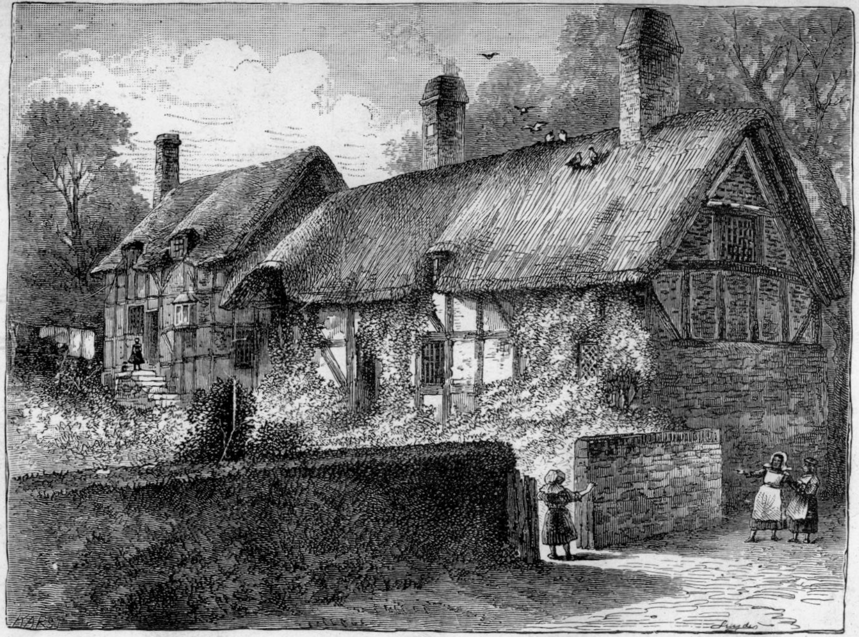

ANNE HATHAWAY'S COTTAGE

Seneca doth counsel thee all swearing to refrain,
Although great profit by it thou might gain;
Pericles, whose words are manifest and plain,
From swearing admonisheth thee to abstain;
The law of God and commandment he gave
Swearing amongst us in no wise would have.
The counsel of philosophers I have here exprest,
Amongst whom swearing was utterly detest;
Much less among Christians ought it to be used,
But utterly of them clean to be refused."

There are also admonitions "against the vice of filthy talking" and "against the vice of lying"; and a prayer follows, " to be said when thou goest to bed."

The rules laid down in the *Boke of Nurture* are similar and in the same doggerel measure. It is interesting, by the bye, to compare the alterations in successive editions as indicating changes in the manners and customs of the time. A single illustration must suffice.

When the first edition appeared, handkerchiefs had not come into general use; and how to blow the nose without one was evidently a difficulty with the writer and other early authorities on deportment. Even in 1577, when handkerchiefs began to be common, Rhodes says :—

"Blow not your nose on the napkin
　　Where you should wipe your hand,
　　But cleanse it in your handkercher." *

* The spelling *handkercher*, common in these old books, and in the early editions of Shakespeare, indicates the pronunciation of the time. In *As You Like It*, *The Taming of the Shrew*, *Hamlet*, *Othello*, and other plays, *napkin* is equivalent to *handkerchief*. This, indeed, is the only meaning of the word in Shakespeare, as often in other writers of the period.

5

The *Booke of Demeanor*, printed in 1619, says:—

> " Nor imitate with Socrates
>   To wipe thy snivelled nose
> Upon thy cap, as he would do,
>   Nor yet upon thy clothes :
> But keep it clean with handkerchief,
>   Provided for the same,
> Not with thy fingers or thy sleeve,
>   Therein thou art to blame."

The introduction of toothpicks, the gradual adoption of forks, already referred to, and sundry other refinements, can be similarly traced in these interesting handbooks.

It would appear that this *Schoole of Vertue*, or some other book with the same title, was used in schools for boys. John Brinsley, in his *Grammar Schoole* of 1612 (quoted by Dr. Furnivall), enumerates the " Bookes to be first learned of children." After mentioning the Primer, the Psalms in metre—" because children will learne that booke with most readinesse and delight through the running of the metre "— and the Testament, he adds : " If any require any other little booke meet to enter children, the *Schoole of Vertue* is one of the principall, and easiest for the first enterers, being full of precepts of civilitie, and such as children will soone learne and take a delight in, thorow [through] the roundnesse of the metre, as was sayde before of the singing Psalmes : and after it the *Schoole of good manners*, called *the new Schoole of Vertue*, leading the childe as by the hand, in the way of all good manners."

INDOOR AMUSEMENTS.

Of the indoor amusements of country people we get an idea from Vincent's *Dialogue with an English Courtier*, published in 1586. He says: "In foul weather we send for some honest neighbors, if haply we be with our wives alone at home (as seldom we are) and with them we play at Dice and Cards, sorting ourselves according to the number of players and their skill; . . . sometimes we fall to Slide-Thrift, to Penny Prick, and in winter nights we use certain Christmas games very proper, and of much agility; we want not also pleasant mad-headed knaves, that be properly learned, and will read in divers pleasant books and good authors; as Sir Guy of Warwick, the Four Sons of Aymon, the Ship of Fools, the Hundred Merry Tales, the Book of Riddles, and many other excellent writers both witty and pleasant. These pretty and pithy matters do sometimes recreate our minds, chiefly after long sitting and loss of money."

"Slide-thrift," called also "slip-groat" and "shove-groat," is a game frequently mentioned by writers of the 16th and 17th centuries. Strutt, in his *Sports and Pastimes of England*, describes it thus:—

"It requires a parallelogram to be made with chalk, or by lines cut upon the middle of a table, about twelve or fourteen inches in breadth, and three or four feet in length: which is divided, latitudinally, into nine sections, in every one of which is placed a figure, in regular succession from one to nine. Each of the players provides himself with a smooth halfpenny, which he places upon the edge of the table, and, striking it with the palm of his hand, drives it towards the marks; and according to the value of the figure affixed to the partition wherein the halfpenny rests, his game is reckoned; which generally is stated at thirty-one, and must be made precisely: if it be exceeded, the player goes again for nine, which must also be brought exactly or the turn is forfeited; and if the halfpenny rests upon any of the marks that separate the partitions, or overpasses the external boundaries, the go is void. It is also to be observed that the players toss up to deter-

SHILLING OF EDWARD VI

mine which shall go first, which is certainly a great advantage."

Shovel-board, or shuffle-board, which some writers confound with slide-thrift, was also played upon a table with coins or flat pieces of metal; but the board was longer and the rules of the game were different.

In 2 *Henry IV.* (ii. 4. 206), when Falstaff wants Pistol put out of the room, he says to Bardolph: "Quoit him down, Bardolph, like a shove-groat shilling."

In *The Merry Wives of Windsor* (i. 1. 159), Slender, when asked if Pistol had picked his purse, replies:

" Ay, by these gloves, did he . . . of seven groats in mill-sixpences and two Edward shovel-boards, that cost me two shillings and twopence apiece." "Edward shovel-boards" were the broad shillings of Edward VI. which were generally used in playing the game. It has been suggested that Slender was a fool to pay two shillings and twopence for a shilling worn smooth; but it is possible that these old coins commanded a premium on account of being in demand for this game. The silver groat (fourpence) was originally used for the purpose, but the shilling, especially of this particular coinage, came to be preferred by players. Taylor the Water Poet makes one of these coins say :—

" You see my face is beardless, smooth, and plain,
    Because my sovereign was a child 't is known,
    When as he did put on the English crown ;
    But had my stamp been bearded, as with hair,
    Long before this it had been worn out bare ;
    For why, with me the unthrifts every day,
    With my face downward, do at shove-board play."

" Penny-prick " is described as " a game consisting of casting oblong pieces of iron at a mark." Another writer explains it as " throwing at halfpence placed on sticks which are called hobs." It was a common game as early as the fifteenth century, and is reproved by a religious writer of that period, probably because it was used for gambling.

Card-playing had become so general in the time of Henry VIII. that a statute was enacted forbidding apprentices to use cards except in the Christmas holidays, and then only in their masters' houses. Many different games with cards are mentioned by writers of the time, but few of them are described minutely enough to make it clear how they were played.

Backgammon, or "tables," as it was called, was popular in Shakespeare's time. He refers to it in *Love's Labour 's Lost* (v. 2, 326), where Biron, ridiculing Boyet, says :—

> " This is the ape of form, monsieur the nice,
> That, when he plays at tables, chides the dice
> In honourable terms."

"Tick-tack" was a kind of backgammon; alluded to, figuratively, in *Measure for Measure* (i. 2. 196): "thus foolishly lost at a game of tick-tack."

"Tray-trip" was a game of dice, in which success depended upon throwing a "tray" (the French *trois*, or three); mentioned in *Twelfth Night* (ii. 5. 207): "Shall I play my freedom at tray-trip, and become thy bond-slave ?"

"Troll-my-dames" was a game resembling the modern bagatelle. The name is a corruption of the French *trou-madame*. It was also known as "pigeon-holes." Dr. John Jones, in his *Ancient Baths of Buck-stone* (1572) refers to it thus: " The ladies, gentlewomen, wives and maids, may in one of the galleries walk; and if the weather be not agreeable to their expectation, they may have in the end of a bench eleven holes made, into the which to troll pummets, or bowls of lead, big, little, or mean, or also of copper, tin, wood, either violent or soft, after their own discretion : the pastime *troule-in-madame* is called."

In *The Tempest* (v. 1. 172) Ferdinand and Miranda

are represented as playing chess; but there is no other clear allusion to the game in Shakespeare's works. It was introduced into England before the Norman Conquest, and became a favorite pastime with the upper classes, but appears to have been little known among the common people.

POPULAR BOOKS.

Of books there were probably very few at the house in Henley Street. Some of those mentioned by Vincent were popular with all classes. The story of Guy of Warwick had been told repeatedly in prose and verse from the twelfth century down to Shakespeare's day, and some of the books and ballads would be likely to be well known in Stratford, which, as we have seen, was in the immediate vicinity of the hero's legendary exploits. The *Four Sons of Aymon* was the translation of a French prose romance, the earliest form of which dated back to songs or ballads of the 13th century. Aymon, or Aimon, a prince of Ardennes whose history was partly imaginary, and his sons figure in the works of Tasso and Ariosto, and other Italian and French poets and romancers.

The *Hundred Merry Tales* was a popular jest-book of Shakespeare's time, to which he alludes in *Much Ado About Nothing* (ii. 1. 134), where Beatrice refers to what Benedick had said about her: "That I was disdainful, and that I had my wit out of the Hundred Merry Tales."

The *Book of Riddles* was another book mentioned by Shakespeare in *The Merry Wives of Windsor* (i. 1. 205), in connection with a volume of verse which was equally popular in the Elizabethan age:—

" *Slender.* I had rather than forty shillings, I had my book of Songs and Sonnets here.—

Enter Simple.

How now, Simple! Where have you been? I must wait on myself, must I? You have not the Book of Riddles about you, have you?

Simple. Book of Riddles? why, did you not lend it to Alice Shortcake upon Allhallowmas last, a fortnight afore Michaelmas?"

The title-page of one edition reads thus: "The Booke of Merry Riddles. Together with proper Questions, and witty Proverbs to make pleasant pastime. No lesse usefull than behoovefull for any yong man or child, to know if he bee quick-witted, or no."

A few of the shortest riddles may be quoted as samples :—

" *The* li. *Riddle.*—My lovers will
        I am content for to fulfill ;
        Within this rime his name is framed ;
        Tell me then how he is named ?

Solution.—His name is William ; for in the first line is *will*, and in the beginning of the second line is *I am*, and then put them both together, and it maketh *William*.

The liv. *Riddle.*—How many calves tailes will reach to the skye? *Solution.*—One, if it be long enough.

The lxv. *Riddle.*—What is that, round as a ball,
        Longer than Pauls steeple, weather-
        cocke, and all ?

Solution.—It is a round bottome of thred when it is unwound.

The lxvii. *Riddle.*—What is that, that goeth thorow the wood, and toucheth never a twig ? *Solution.*—It is the blast of a horne, or any other noyse."

A *bottom* of thread was a ball of it. The word occurs in *The Taming of the Shrew* (iv. 3. 138), where Grumio says, in the dialogue with the Tailor : " Master, if ever I said loose-bodied gown, sew me in the skirts of it, and beat me to death with a bottom of brown thread ; I said a gown." The verb is used in *The Two Gentlemen of Verona* (iii. 2. 53):—

> " Therefore, as you unwind her love from him,
> Lest it should ravel and be good to none,
> You must provide to bottom it on me."

This old meaning of *bottom* doubtless suggested the name of Bottom the Weaver in the *Midsummer-Night's Dream*.

STORY-TELLING.

If books were scarce in the homes of the common people when Shakespeare was a boy, there was no lack of oral tales, legends, and folk-lore for the entertainment of the family of a winter evening. The store of this unwritten history and fiction was inexhaustible.

In Milton's *L'Allegro* we have a pleasant picture of a rustic group listening to fairy stories round the evening fire :—

> " Then to the spicy nut-brown ale,
> With stories told of many a feat,
> How fairy Mab the junkets eat.
> She was pinch'd and pull'd, she said,
> And he, by Friar's lantern led,

Tells how the drudging goblin sweat
To earn his cream-bowl duly set,
When in one night, ere glimpse of morn,
His shadowy flail hath thresh'd the corn
That ten day-laborers could not end ;
Then lies him down the lubber fiend,
And, stretch'd out all the chimney's length,
Basks at the fire his hairy strength,
And crop-full out of doors he flings
Ere the first cock his matin rings.
Thus done the tales, to bed they creep,
By whispering winds soon lull'd asleep."

Of "fairy Mab" we have a graphic description from
the merry Mercutio in *Romeo and Juliet* (i. 4. 53–94) ;
and the "drudging goblin," or Robin Goodfellow, is
the Puck of the *Midsummer-Night's Dream*, to whom
the Fairy says (ii. 1. 40) :—

"Those that Hobgoblin call you and sweet Puck,
You do their work, and they shall have good luck."

In the same scene Puck himself tells of the practical
jokes he plays upon "the wisest aunt telling the sad-
dest tale" to a fireside group, and of many another
sportive trick with which he "frights the maidens" and
vexes the housewives.

The children had their stories to tell, like their elders ;
and Shakespeare has pictured a home scene in *The
Winter's Tale* (ii. 1. 21) which may have been suggest-
ed by his own experience as a boy. As Mr. Charles
Knight asks, "may we not read for Hermione, Mary
Shakespeare, and for Mamillius, William ?"

"*Hermione.* What wisdom stirs amongst you ? Come,
    sir, now
I am for you again ; pray you, sit by us,
And tell 's a tale.
    Mamillius.   Merry, or sad shall 't be ?
    Hermione. As merry as you will.
    Mamillius. A sad tale 's best for winter. I have one
Of sprites and goblins.
    Hermione.   Let 's have that, good sir.
Come on, sit down ; come on, and do your best
To fright me with your sprites ; you 're powerful at it.
    Mamillius. There was a man—
    Hermione.   Nay, come, sit down ; then on.
    Mamillius. Dwelt by a churchyard :—I will tell it softly ;
Yond crickets shall not hear it.
    Hermione.   Come on, then,
And give 't me in mine ear."

Just then his father, Leontes, comes in, and the tale is
interrupted, never to be resumed.

Mr. Knight assumes, with a good degree of probability, that William had access to some of the books
from which he drew material for the story of his plays
later in life, and that he may have told these tales,
whether "merry or sad," to his brothers and sisters at
home.

"He had," says this genial biographer, "a copy, well
thumbed from his first reading days, of 'The Palace of
Pleasure, beautified, adorned, and well furnished with
pleasant histories and excellent novelles, selected out
of divers good and commendable authors ; by William
Painter, Clarke of the Ordinaunce and Armarie.' In
this book, according to the dedication of the translator
to Ambrose Earl of Warwick, was set forth 'the great
valiance of noble gentlemen, the terrible combats of

courageous personages, the virtuous minds of noble dames, the chaste hearts of constant ladies, the wonderful patience of puissant princes, the mild sufferance of well-disposed gentlewomen, and, in divers, the quiet bearing of adverse fortune.' Pleasant little apothegms and short fables were there in the book ; which the brothers and sisters of William Shakespeare had heard him tell with marvellous spirit, and they abided therefore in their memories. There was Æsop's fable of the old lark and her young ones, wherein 'he prettily and aptly doth premonish that hope and confidence of things attempted by man ought to be fixed and trusted in none other but himself.' There was the story, most delightful to a child, of the bondman at Rome, who was brought into the open place upon which a great multitude looked, to fight with a lion of a marvellous bigness ; and the fierce lion, when he saw him, 'suddenly stood still, and afterwards by little and little, in gentle sort, he came unto the man as though he had known him,' and licked his hands and legs ; and the bondman told that he had healed in former time the wounded foot of the lion, and the beast became his friend. These were for the younger children ; but William had now a new tale, out of the same storehouse, upon which he had often pondered, the subject of which had shaped itself in his mind into dialogue that almost sounded like verse in his graceful and earnest recitation. It was a tale which Painter translated from the French of Pierre Boisteau. . . . It was 'The goodly history of the true and constant love between Romeo and Julietta.' . . . From the same collection of tales had the youth before half dramatized the story of 'Giletta of Narbonne,' who cured the King of France of a painful malady, and the king gave her in marriage to the Count Beltramo, with whom she had been brought up, and her husband despised and forsook her, but at last they were united, and lived in great honor and felicity.

"There was another collection, too, which that youth had diligently read, — the 'Gesta Romanorum,' translated by R. Robinson in 1577,—old legends, come down to those latter days from monkish historians, who had embodied in their narratives all the wild traditions of the ancient and modern world. He could tell the story of the rich heiress who chose a husband by the machinery of a gold, a silver, and a leaden casket; and another story of the merchant whose inexorable creditor required the fulfilment of his bond in cutting a pound of flesh, nearest the merchant's heart, and by the skilful interpretation of the bond the cruel creditor was defeated.

"There was the story, too, in these legends, of the Emperor Theodosius, who had three daughters ; and those two daughters who said they loved him more than themselves were unkind to him, but the youngest, who only said she loved him as much as he was worthy, succoured him in his need, and was his true daughter. . . .

"Stories such as these, preserved amidst the wreck of time, were to that youth like the seeds that are found in the tombs of ruined cities, lying with the bones of forgotten generations, but which the genial influence of nature will call into life, and they shall become flowers, and trees, and food for man.

"But, beyond all these, our Mamillius had many a tale 'of sprites and goblins' . . . Such appearances were above nature, but the commonest movements of the natural world had them in subjection :—

" 'I have heard,
The cock, that is the trumpet to the morn,
Doth with his lofty and shrill-sounding throat
Awake the god of day; and at his warning,
Whether in sea or fire, in earth or air,
The extravagant and erring spirit hies
To his confine.'

" Powerful they were, but yet powerless. They came
for benevolent purposes : to warn the guilty; to discover the guilt. The belief in them was not a debasing
thing. It was associated with the enduring confidence
that rested upon a world beyond this material world.
Love hoped for such visitations; it had its dreams of
such—where the loved one looked smilingly, and spoke
of regions where change and separation were not. They
might be talked of, even among children then, without
terror. They lived in that corner of the soul which had
trust in angel protections, which believed in celestial
hierarchies, which listened to hear the stars moving in
harmonious music. . . .

" William Shakespeare could also tell to his greedy
listeners, how in the old days of King Arthur

" 'The elf-queene, with her jolly compagnie,
Danced full oft in many a grene mede.'

" Here was something in his favorite old poet for the
youth to work out into beautiful visions of a pleasant
race of supernatural beings ; who lived by day in the
acorn cups of Arden, and by moonlight held their
revels on the greensward of Avon-side, the ringlets
of their dance being duly seen, 'whereof the ewe not
bites'; who tasted the honey-bag of the bee, and held

counsel by the light of the glowworm; who kept the
cankers from the rosebuds, and silenced the hootings
of the owl. . . . Some day would William make a little
play of Fairies, and Joan should be their Queen, and he
would be the King; for he had talked with the Fairies,
and he knew their language and their manners, and
they were 'good people,' and would not mind a boy's
sport with them.

"But when the youth began to speak of witches there
was fear and silence. For did not his mother recollect
that in the year she was married Bishop Jewell had told
the Queen that her subjects pined away, even unto the
death, and that their affliction was owing to the increase of witches and sorcerers? Was it not known
how there were three sorts of witches,—those that can
hurt and not help, those that can help and not hurt,
and those that can both help and hurt? It was unsafe
even to talk of them.

"But the youth had met with the history of the murder
of Duncan King of Scotland, in a chronicler older than
Holinshed; and he told softly, so that 'yon crickets
shall not hear it,' that, as Macbeth and Banquo journeyed from Forres, sporting by the way together,
when the warriors came in the midst of a laund,
three weird sisters suddenly appeared to them, in
strange and wild apparel, resembling creatures of
an elder world, and prophesied that Macbeth should
be King of Scotland; and Macbeth from that hour
desired to be king, and so killed the good king his
liege lord.

"And then the story-teller would pass on to safer
matters—to the calculations of learned men who could
read the fates of mankind in the aspects of the stars;

and of those more deeply learned, clothed in garments of white linen, who had command over the spirits of the earth, of the water, and of the air. Some of the children said that a horseshoe over the door, and vervain and dill, would preserve them, as they had been told, from the devices of sorcery. But their mother called to their mind that there was security far more to be relied on than charms of herb or horseshoe — that there was a Power that would preserve them from all evil, seen or unseen, if such were His gracious will, and if they humbly sought Him, and offered up their hearts to Him in all love and trust. And to that Power this household then addressed themselves; and the night was without fear, and their sleep was pleasant."

CHRISTENINGS.

In the olden time the christening of a child was an occasion of feasting and gift-giving. It was an ancient custom for the sponsors to make a present of silver or gilt spoons to the infant. These were called "apostle spoons," because the end of the handle was formed into the figure of one of the apostles. The rich or generous gave the whole twelve; those less wealthy or liberal limited themselves to the four evangelists; while the poor contented themselves with the gift of a single spoon.

There is an allusion to this custom in *Henry VIII.* (v. 3. 168), where the King replies to Cranmer, who has professed to be unworthy of being a sponsor to the baby Elizabeth, "Come, come, my lord, you'd spare your spoons," — a playful insinuation that the archbishop wants to escape making a present to the child.

It is related that Shakespeare was godfather to one of Ben Jonson's children, and said to his friend after the christening, "I' faith, Ben, I'll e'en give him a dozen

ANCIENT FONT AT STRATFORD

good Latin spoons, and thou shalt translate them.' That is, as Mr. Thoms explains it, " Shakespeare, willing to show his wit, if not his wealth, gave a dozen spoons, not of silver, but of *latten*, a name formerly used to signify a mixed metal resembling brass, as being the most appropriate gift to the child of a father so learned."

After baptism at the church a piece of white linen was put upon the head of the child. This was called the "chrisom" or "chrisom-cloth," and originally was worn seven days; but after the Reformation it was

6

kept on until the churching of the mother. If the child died before the churching, it was buried with the chrisom upon it. In parish registers such infants are often referred to as "chrisoms." In *Henry V.* (ii. 3. 12), Dame Quickly says of Falstaff, "A' made a finer end, and went away an it had been any christom child"; that is, his death was like that of a young infant. "Christom" is the old woman's blunder for "chrisom."

The "bearing-cloth" was the mantle which covered the child when it was carried to the font. In the *Winter's Tale* (iii. 3. 119), the Shepherd, when he finds the infant Perdita abandoned on the sea-shore, says to his son: "Here's a sight for thee; look thee, a bearing-cloth for a squire's child! Look thee here; take up, take up, boy; open 't." John Stow, writing in the closing years of the 16th century, says that at that time it was not customary "for godfathers and godmothers generally to give plate at the baptism of children, but only to give 'christening shirts,' with little bands and cuffs, wrought either with silk or blue thread. The best of them, for chief persons, were edged with a small lace of black silk and gold, the highest price of which, for great men's children, was seldom above a noble [a gold coin worth 6*s*. 8*d*.], and the common sort, two, three, or four, and six shillings apiece."

The "gossips' feast" (or sponsors' feast) held in honor of those who were associated in the christening, was an ancient English custom often mentioned by dramatists and other writers of the Elizabethan age. In the *Comedy of Errors* (v. 1. 405) the Abbess, when she finds that the twin brothers Antipholus are her long-lost sons, says to the company present:—

" Thirty-three years have I but gone in travail
Of you, my sons; and till this present hour
My heavy burthen ne'er delivered.—
The duke, my husband, and my children both,
And you the calendars of their nativity,
Go to a gossip's feast, and go with me;
After so long grief, such nativity !"

And the Duke replies, " With all my heart I'll gossip at this feast."

In the *Bachelor's Banquet* (1603) we find an allusion to these feasts: " What cost and trouble will it be to have all things fine against the Christening Day; what store of sugar, biscuits, comfets, and caraways, marmalet, and marchpane, with all kinds of sweet-suckers and superfluous banqueting stuff, with a hundred other odd and needless trifles, which at that time must fill the pockets of dainty dames." It would appear from this that the women at the feast not only ate what they pleased, but carried off some of the good things in their pockets.

A writer in 1666, alluding to this and the falling-off in the custom of giving presents at christenings, says :—

' Especially since gossips now
Eat more at christenings than bestow.
Formerly when they used to trowl
Gilt bowls of sack, they gave the bowl—
Two spoons at least; an use ill kept:
'T is well now if our own be left."

He insinuates that some of the guests were as likely to steal spoons from the table as to give gilt bowls or "apostle spoons" to the infant.

The boy Shakespeare must have often seen this ceremony of christening. His sister Joan was baptized when he was five years old; his sister Anna when he was eight; his brother Richard when he was ten; and Edmund when he was sixteen.

SUPERSTITIONS CONNECTED WITH BIRTH AND BAPTISM.

In the time of Shakespeare babies were supposed to be exposed to other risks and dangers than the infantile disorders to which they are subject. Mary Shakespeare, as she watched the cradle of the infant William, may have been troubled by fears and anxieties that never occur to a fond mother now.

Witches and fairies were supposed to be given to stealing beautiful and promising children, and substituting their own ugly and mischievous offspring. Shakespeare alludes to these "changelings," as they were called, in the *Midsummer-Night's Dream* (ii. 1. 23), where Puck says that Oberon is angry with Titania

> " Because that she as her attendant hath
> A lovely boy, stolen from an Indian king;
> She never had so sweet a changeling."

This "changeling boy" is alluded to several times afterwards in the play.

In the *Winter's Tale* (iii. 3. 122), when the Shepherd finds Perdita, he says: "It was told me I should be rich by the fairies; this is some changeling"; and the money left with the infant he believes to be "fairy gold." As the child is beautiful he does not take it to

be one of the ugly elves left in exchange for a stolen
babe, but a human changeling which the fairy thieves
have for some reason abandoned. If it were not for
the gold left with it, he might suppose that the stolen
infant had been temporarily hidden there. We have
an allusion to such behavior on the part of the fairies
in Spenser's *Faerie Queene* (i. 10. 65) :—

" For well I wote thou springst from ancient race
  Of Saxon kinges, that have with mightie hand,
  And many bloody battailes fought in face,
  High reard their royall throne in Britans land,
  And vanquisht them, unable to withstand :
  From thence a Faery thee unweeting reft,
  There as thou slepst in tender swadling band,
  And her base Elfin brood there for thee left :
  Such men do Chaungelings call, so chaung'd by
      Faeries theft.

Thence she thee brought into this Faery lond [land]
  And in a heaped furrow did thee hyde ;
  Where thee a Ploughman all unweeting fond [found]
  As he his toylesome teme that way did guyde,
  And brought thee up in a ploughmans state to byde."

In 1 *Henry IV.* (i. 1. 87), the King, contrasting the
gallant Hotspur with his own profligate son, exclaims :

      " O that it could be proved
  That some night-tripping fairy had exchang'd
  In cradle-clothes our children where they lay,
  And call'd mine Percy, his Plantagenet !
  Then would I have his Harry, and he mine."

The belief in the " evil eye " was another superstition prevalent in Shakespeare's day, as it had been

from the earliest times. It dates back to old Greek and Roman days, being mentioned by Theocritus, Virgil, and other classical writers. In Turkey passages from the Koran used to be painted on the outside of houses as a protection against this malignant influence of witches, who were supposed to cause serious injury to human beings and animals by merely looking at them.

Thomas Lupton, in his *Book of Notable Things* (1586) says: "The eyes be not only instruments of enchantment, but also the voice and evil tongues of certain persons." Bacon, in one of his minor works, remarks: "It seems some have been so curious as to note that the times when the stroke or percussion of an envious eye does most hurt are particularly when the party envied is beheld in glory and triumph."

Robert Heron, writing in 1793 of his travels in Scotland, says: "Cattle are subject to be injured by what is called an *evil eye*, for some persons are supposed to have naturally a blasting power in their eyes, with which they injure whatever offends or is hopelessly desired by them. Witches and warlocks are also much disposed to wreak their malignity on cattle. . . . It is common to bind into a cow's tail a small piece of mountain-ash wood, as a charm against witchcraft."

As recently as August, 1839, a London newspaper reports a case in which a woman was suspected of the evil eye by a fellow-lodger merely because she squinted.

In this case, as in many others, the possession of the evil eye may not have been supposed due to any evil purpose or character. Good people might be born with this baleful influence, and might exert it against

their will or even unconsciously. It is said that Pius
IX., soon after his election as Pope, when he was perhaps the best loved man in Italy, happened while passing through the streets in his carriage to glance up-
ward at an open window at which a nurse was standing with a child. A few minutes afterward the nurse
let the child drop and it was killed. Nobody thought
that the Pope wished this, but the fancy that he
had the evil eye became universal and lasted till his
death.

In the *Merry Wives of Windsor* (v. 5. 87) Pistol
says to Falstaff: "Vile worm, thou wast o'erlook'd
even in thy birth." In the *Merchant of Venice* (iii. 2.
15) Portia playfully refers to the same superstition in
talking with Bassanio :—

> " Beshrew your eyes,
> They have o'erlook'd me and divided me ;
> One half of me is yours, the other half yours."

CHARMS AND AMULETS.

Against these dangers, and many like them which it
would take an entire volume to enumerate, protection
was sought by charms and amulets. These were also
supposed to prevent or cure certain diseases. Magicians and witches employed charms to accomplish their
evil purposes ; and other charms were used to thwart
these purposes by those who feared mischief from
them.

In *Othello* (i. 2. 62) Brabantio, the father of Desdemona, suspects that the Moor has won his daughter's
love by charms. He says to Othello :—

" O thou foul thief, where hast thou stow'd my daughter?
Damn'd as thou art, thou hast enchanted her."

In the preceding scene, talking with Roderigo, he
asks :—

> " Is there not charms
> By which the property of youth and maidhood
> May be abused? Have you not heard, Roderigo,
> Of some such thing?"

And Roderigo replies: "Yes, sir, I have indeed."
When Othello afterward tells how he had gained the
maiden's love, he says in conclusion :—

> " She loved me for the dangers I had pass'd,
> And I loved her that she did pity them.
> This only is the witchcraft I have used."

In the *Midsummer-Night's Dream* (i. 1. 27) Egeus
accuses Lysander of wooing Hermia by magic arts:
" This man hath bewitch'd the bosom of my child."

In *Much Ado About Nothing* (iii. 2. 72) Benedick,
when his friends banter him for pretending to have
the toothache, replies: " Yet this is no charm for the
toothache."

John Melton, in his *Astròlogaster* (1620), says it is
vulgarly believed that " toothaches, agues, cramps, and
fevers, and many other diseases may be healed by
mumbling a few strange words over the head of the
diseased."

Written charms in prose or verse—or neither, being
nonsensical combinations of words, letters, or signs—
were in great favor then, as before and since. The
unmeaning word *abracadabra* was much used in in-

PORCH, STRATFORD CHURCH

cantations, and worn as an amulet was supposed to
cure or prevent certain ailments. It was necessary to
write it in the following form, if one would secure its
full potency:—

```
A  B  R  A  C  A  D  A  B  R  A
 A  B  R  A  C  A  D  A  B  R
  A  B  R  A  C  A  D  A  B
   A  B  R  A  C  A  D  A
    A  B  R  A  C  A  D
     A  B  R  A  C  A
      A  B  R  A  C
       A  B  R  A
        A  B  R
         A  B
          A
```

A manuscript in the British Museum contains this
note: "Mr. Banester saith that he healed 200 in one
year of an ague by hanging *abracadabra* about their
necks."

Thomas Lodge, in his *Incarnate Divels* (1596)
refers to written charms thus: "Bring him but a
table [tablet] of lead, with crosses (and 'Adonai' or
'Elohim' written in it), he thinks it will heal the
ague."

Certain trees, like the elder and the ash, were supposed to furnish valuable material for charms and amulets. A writer in 1651 says: "The common people
keep as a great secret the leaves of the elder which
they have gathered the last day of April; which to dis-
appoint the charms of witches they affix to their doors
and windows." An amulet against erysipelas was
made of "elder on which the sun never shined," a

"piece betwixt two knots" being hung about the patient's neck.

In a book published in 1599 it is asserted that "if one eat three small pomegranate-flowers, they say for a whole year he shall be safe from all manner of eye sore." According to the same authority, "it hath been and yet is a thing which superstition hath believed, that the body anointed with the juice of chicory is very available to obtain the favor of great persons."

Wearing a bay-leaf was a charm against lightning. Robert Greene, *Penelope's Web* (1601), says: "He which weareth the bay leaf is privileged from the prejudice of thunder." In Webster's *White Devil* (1612) Cornelia says:—

> "Reach the bays:
> I'll tie a garland here about his head;
> 'T will keep my boy from lightning."

Burton, in his *Anatomy of Melancholy* (1621), remarks: "Amulets, and things to be borne about, I find prescribed, taxed [condemned] by some, approved by others. . . . I say with Renodeus, they are not altogether to be rejected."

Reginald Scot, in his *Discoverie of Witchcraft*, published in 1584, in which he exposed and ridiculed the pretensions of witches, magicians, and astrologers, tells an amusing story of an old woman who cured diseases by muttering a certain form of words over the person afflicted; for which service she always received a penny and a loaf of bread. At length, terrified by threats of being burned as a witch, she owned that her whole conjuration consisted in these lines, which she repeated in a low voice near the head of the patient:—

> " Thy loaf in my hand,
>   And thy penny in my purse,
> Thou art never the better,
>   And I—am never the worse."

Scot was one of the few men of that age who dared to assail the general belief in witchcraft and magic; and James I. ordered his book to be burned by the common hangman. That monarch also wrote his *Demonology*, as he tells us, " chiefly against the damnable opinions of Wierus and Scot; the latter of whom is not ashamed in public print to deny there can be such a thing as witchcraft." Eminent divines and scientific writers joined in the attempt to refute this bold attack upon the ignorance and superstition of the time.

We infer, from certain passages in the plays, that Shakespeare had read Scot's book; and we have good reason to believe that, like Scot, he was far enough in advance of his age to see the absurdity of the popular faith in magic and witchcraft. In his boyhood we may suppose that he believed in 'them, as his parents and everybody in Stratford doubtless did; but when he became a man he appears to have regarded them only as curious old folk - lore from which he could now and then draw material for use in his plays and poems.

The illustrations here given of the vulgar superstitions of Shakespeare's time are merely a few out of thousands equally interesting to be found in books on the subject, or scattered through the dramatic and other literature of the period.

Part III

AT SCHOOL

INNER COURT, GRAMMAR SCHOOL

THE STRATFORD GRAMMAR SCHOOL

The Stratford Grammar School, as we have already
seen (page 38 above), was an ancient institution in
Shakespeare's day, having been originally founded in
the first half of the 15th century by the Guild, and,
after the dissolution of that body, created by royal charter, in June, 1553, "The King's New School of Stratford-upon-Avon." The charter describes it as "a cer-

tain free grammar school, to consist of one master and teacher, hereafter for ever to endure." The master was to be appointed by the Earl of Warwick, and was to receive twenty pounds a year from the income of certain lands given by the King for that purpose. A part of the expenses of the school is to this day paid from the same royal endowment.

The school-house stood, as it still does, close beside the Guild Chapel, the school-rooms on the second story being originally reached by an outside staircase, roofed with tile, which was demolished about fifty years ago. The building was old and out of repair in Shakespeare's boyhood. In 1568 it was partially renovated, and while the work was going on the school was transferred to the adjoining chapel, as it may have been under similar cir-cumstances on more than one former occasion. This probably suggested Shakespeare's comparison of Mal-volio to "a pedant that keeps a school i' the church" (*Twelfth Night*, iii. 2. 80). In 1595 the holding of school in church or chapel was forbidden by statute.

The training in an English free day-school in the time of Elizabeth depended much on the attainments of the master, and these varied greatly, bad teachers being the rule and good ones the exception. "It is a general plague and complaint of the whole land," writes Henry Peacham in the 17th century, "for, for one discreet and able teacher, you shall find twenty ignorant and careless; who (among so many fertile and delicate wits as England affordeth), whereas they make one scholar, they mar ten." Roger Ascham, some years earlier, had written in the same strain. In many towns the office of schoolmaster was conferred on "an ancient citizen of no great learning." Sometimes a quack con-

THE LATIN SCHOOL-ROOM

juring doctor had the position, like Pinch in the *Comedy
of Errors* (v. 1. 237), whom Antipholus of Ephesus describes thus:—

> "Along with them
> They brought one Pinch, a hungry lean-fac'd villain,
> A mere anatomy, a mountebank,
> A threadbare juggler, and a fortune-teller,
> A needy, hollow-eyed, sharp-looking wretch,
> A living dead man. This pernicious slave,
> Forsooth, took on him as a conjurer;

7

> And, gazing in mine eyes, feeling my pulse,
> And with no face, as 't were, out-facing me,
> Cries out, I was possess'd."

Pinch is not called a schoolmaster in the text of the play, but in the stage-direction of the earliest edition (1623) he is described, on his entrance, as "a schoole-master call'd Pinch."

In old times the village pedagogue often had the reputation of being a conjurer; that is, of one who could exorcise evil spirits — perhaps because he was the one man in the village, except the priest, who could speak Latin, the only language supposed to be "understanded of devils."

A certain master of St. Alban's School in the middle of the 16th century declared that "by no entreaty would he teach any scholar he had, further than his father had learned before them," arguing that, if educated beyond that point, they would "prove saucy rogues and control their fathers."

The masters of the Stratford school at the time when Shakespeare probably attended it were university men of at least fair scholarship and ability, as we infer from the fact that they rapidly gained promotion in the church. Thomas Hunt, who was master during the most important years of William's school course, became vicar of the neighboring village of Luddington.   " In the pedantic Holofernes of *Love's Labour's Lost*, Shakespeare has carefully portrayed the best type of the rural schoolmaster, as in Pinch he has portrayed the worst, and the freshness and fulness of detail imparted to the former portrait may easily lead to the conclusion that its author was drawing upon his own experience." We

need not suppose that Holofernes is the exact counter-
part of Master Hunt, but the latter was probably, like
the former, a thorough scholar.

WHAT SHAKESPEARE LEARNT AT SCHOOL.

We may imagine young William wending his way to
the Grammar School for the first time on a May morning in 1571. If he was born on the 23d of April, 1564
(or May 3d, according to our present calendar), he had
now reached the age of seven years, at which he could
enter the school. The only other requirement for ad-
mission, in the case of a Stratford boy, was that he
should be able to read; and this he had probably
learned at home with the aid of a "horn-book," such
as he afterwards referred to in *Love's Labour's Lost*
(v. 1. 49):—

"Yes, yes; he teaches boys the horn-book.
What is a, b, spelt backward with the horn on its head?"

This primer of our forefathers, which continued
in common use in England down to the middle of
the last century at least, was a single printed leaf,
usually set in a frame of wood and covered with a
thin plate of transparent horn, from which it got
its name. There was generally a handle to hold it
by, and through a hole in the handle a cord was put
by which the "book" was slung to the girdle of the
scholar.

In a book printed in 1731 we read of "a child, in a
bodice coat and leading-strings, with a horn-book tied
to her side." In 1715 we find mention of the price of

a horn-book as twopence; but Shakespeare's probably cost only half as much.

The leaf had at the top the alphabet large and small, with a list of the vowels and a string of easy monosyllables of the *ab*, *eb*, *ib* sort, and a copy of the Lord's Prayer. The matter varied somewhat from time to time.

Here is an exact reproduction of the text of one specimen, from a recent catalogue of a London antiquarian bookseller, who prices it at twelve guineas, or a trifle more than sixty dollars. These old horn-books are now excessively rare, having seldom survived the wear and tear of the nursery.

+Aabcdefghijklmnopq
rſstuvwxyz&   aeiou
ABCDEFGHIJKLMNOPQ
RSTUVWXYZ

a e i o u	a e i o u
ab eb ib ob ub	ba be bi bo bu
ac ec ic oc uc	ca ce ci co cu
ad ed id od ud	da de di do du

In the Name of the Father, and of the Son, and of the Holy Ghoſt. *Amen.*

OUR Father, which art in Heaven, hallowed be thy Name; thy Kingdom come, thy Will be done on Earth, as it is in Heaven. Give us this Day our daily Bread; and forgive us our treſpaſſes, as we forgive them that treſpaſs againſt us: And lead us not into Temptation, but deliver us from Evil. *Amen.*

The alphabet was prefaced by a cross, whence it came to be called the Christ Cross row,* corrupted into "criss-cross-row" or contracted into "cross-row"; as in *Richard III.* (i. 1. 55), where Clarence says :—

> "He harkens after prophecies and dreams,
> And from the cross-row plucks the letter G,
> And says a wizard told him that by G
> His issue disinherited should be."

Shenstone alludes to the horn-book in *The School-mistress* :—

> "Their books of stature small they take in hand,
> Which with pellucid horn secured are
> To save from fingers wet the letters fair."

Possibly, the boy William, instead of a horn-book, had an "A-B-C book," which often contained a cate-chism, in addition to the elementary reading matter. To this we have an allusion in *King John*, i. 1. 196:—

> "Now your traveller—
> He and his toothpick at my worship's mess,
> And when my knightly stomach is sufficed,
> Why, then I suck my teeth and catechise
> My picked man of countries : 'My dear sir,'—
> Thus, leaning on my elbow, I begin,—
> 'I shall beseech you'—that is question now;
> And then comes answer like an Absey book."

* Some believe it got the name from having the letters arranged in the form of a cross, as they sometimes were ; but the other explanation seems to me the more probable.

" Absey " is one of many old spellings for " A-B-C "
—*abece, apece, apecy, apsie, absee, abcee, abeesee,* etc.

It was not a long walk that our seven-year-old boy
had to take in going to school. Turning the corner of
Henley Street, where his father lives (compare the
map, page 42 above), he passes into the High Street,
on which (though the street changes its name twice
before we get there) the Guildhall is situated. The
adjoining Guild Chapel is separated only by a nar-

row lane from the "great
house," as it was called,
the handsomest in all
Stratford.

The child, as he passes
that grand mansion, little
dreams that, some twenty-
five years later, he will
buy it for his own resi-
dence.

DESK SAID TO BE SHAKESPEARE'S

The Latin room (page 97) probably looks to-day very
much as it did when William studied there, the modern
plastered ceiling which hid the oak roof of the olden
time having been removed. The wainscoted walls,
with the small windows high above the floor, are evidently ancient. A desk which was formerly in this
room, and said (with no authority whatever) to have
been used by Shakespeare, is preserved in the Henley
Street house. An adjacent room is known as the
"mathematical room," and a smaller one on the same
floor is used for the library.

What did William study in the Grammar School?
Not much except arithmetic and Latin, with perhaps a
little Greek and a mere smattering of other branches.

His first lessons in Latin were probably from two well-known books of the time, the *Accidence* and the *Sententiæ Pueriles*. The examination of Master Page by the Welsh parson and schoolmaster, Sir Hugh Evans, in *The Merry Wives of Windsor* (iv. 1) is taken almost verbally from the *Accidence*. Mrs. Page, accompanied by her son and the illiterate Dame Quickly, meets Sir Hugh in the street, and this dialogue ensues :—

" *Mrs. Page.* How now, Sir Hugh ! no school to-day ?

Evans. No ; master Slender is get the boys leave to play.

Quickly. Blessing of his heart !

Mrs. Page. Sir Hugh, my husband says, my son profits nothing in the world at his book. I pray you, ask him some questions in his accidence.

Evans. Come hither, William ; hold up your head ; come.

Mrs. Page. Come on, sirrah ; hold up your head ; answer your master, be not afraid.

Evans. William, how many numbers is in nouns ?

William. Two.

Quickly. Truly, I thought there had been one number more, because they say, 'od's nouns.

Evans. Peace your tattlings !—What is *fair*, William ?

William. Pulcher.

Quickly. Pole-cats ! there are fairer things than pole-cats, sure.

Evans. You are a very simplicity 'oman ; I pray you peace.—What is *lapis*, William ?

William. A stone.

Evans. And what is a stone, William ?

William. A pebble.

Evans. No, it is *lapis :* I pray you remember in your prain.

William. Lapis.

Evans. That is a good William. What is he, William, that does lend articles?

William. Articles are borrowed of the pronoun; and be thus declined, *Singulariter, nominativo, hic, hæc, hoc.*

Evans. Nominativo, hig, hag, hog; — pray you, mark: *genitivo, hujus.* Well, what is your accusative case?

William. Accusativo, hinc.

Evans. I pray you, have your remembrance, child; *accusativo, hung, hang, hog.*

Quickly. Hang-hog is Latin for bacon, I warrant you.

Evans. Leave your prabbles, 'oman.—What is the focative case, William?

William. O!—*vocativo,* O!.

Evans. Remember, William; focative is *caret.*

Quickly. And that's a good root.

Evans. 'Oman, forbear.

Mrs. Page. Peace!

*   *   *   *   *   *   *

Quickly. You do ill to teach the child such words.—He teaches him to hick and to hack, which they'll do fast enough of themselves. Fie upon you!

Evans. 'Oman, art thou lunatics? hast thou no understandings for thy cases, and the numbers of the genders? Thou art as foolish Christian creatures as I would desires.

Mrs. Page. Prithee, hold thy peace.

Evans. Show me now, William, some declensions of your pronouns.

William. Forsooth, I have forgot.

Evans. It is *qui, quæ, quod;* if you forget your *quis,* your *quæs,* and your *quods,* you must be preeches. Go your ways, and play; go.

Mrs. Page. He is a better scholar than I thought he was.

Evans. He is a good sprag memory. Farewell, mistress Page.

Mrs. Page. Adieu, good Sir Hugh."

The *Sententiæ Pueriles* was a collection of brief sentences from many authors, including moral and religious passages intended for the use of the boys on Saints' days.

The Latin Grammar studied by William was certainly Lilly's, the standard manual of the time, as long before and after. The first edition was published in 1513, and one was issued as late as 1817, or more than three hundred years afterward. In *The Taming of the Shrew* (i. 1. 167) a passage from Terence is quoted in the modified form in which it appears in this grammar.

There are certain people, by the way, who believe that Shakespeare's plays were written by Francis Bacon. Can we imagine the sage of St. Albans, familiar as he was with classical literature, going to his old Latin Grammar for a quotation from Terence, and not to the original works of that famous playwright?

In *Love's Labour's Lost* (iv. 2. 95) Holofernes quotes the "good old Mantuan," as he calls him, the passage being evidently a reminiscence of Shakespeare's schoolboy Latin. The "Mantuan" is not Virgil, as one might at first suppose (and as Mr. Andrew Lang, who is a good scholar, assumes in his pleasant comments on the play in *Harper's Magazine* for May, 1893), but Baptista Mantuanus, or Giovanni Battista Spagnuoli (or Spagnoli), who got the name Mantuanus from his birthplace.

He died in 1516, less than fifty years before Shakespeare was born, and was the author of sundry *Eclogues*, which the pedants of that day preferred to Virgil's, and which were much read in schools. The first Eclogue begins with the passage quoted by Holofernes.

A little earlier in the same scene the old pedant

gives us a quotation from Lilly's Grammar. Other bits
of Latin with which he interlards his talk are taken,
with little or no variation, from the *Sententiæ Pueriles*
or similar Elizabethan phrase-books.

THE NEGLECT OF ENGLISH.

No English was taught in the Stratford school
then, or for many years after. It is only in our own
day that it has begun to receive proper attention in
schools of this grade in England, or indeed in our own
country.

It is interesting, however, to know that the first English schoolmaster to urge the study of the vernacular
tongue was a contemporary of Shakespeare. In 1561
Richard Mulcaster, who had been educated at King's
College, Cambridge, and Christ Church, Oxford, was
appointed head-master of Merchant-Taylors School in
London, which had just been founded as a feeder, or
preparatory school, for St. John's College, Oxford. In
his *Elementarie*, published in 1582, he has the following
plea for the study of English :—

"But because I take upon me in this Elementarie,
besides some friendship to secretaries for the pen, and
to correctors for the print, to direct such people as
teach children to read and write English, and the *reading* must needs be such as the writing leads unto, therefore, before I meddle with any particular precept, to
direct the reader, I will thoroughly rip up the whole
certainty of our English writing, so far forth and with
such assurance as probability can make me, because it
is a thing both proper to my argument and profitable
to my country. For our natural tongue being as bene-

ficial unto us for our needful delivery as any other is to the people which use it; and having as pretty and as fair observations in it as any other hath; and being as ready to yield to any rule of art as any other is; why should I not take some pains to find out the right writing of ours as other countrymen have done to find the like in theirs? and so much the rather because it is pretended that the writing thereof is marvellous uncertain, and scant to be recovered from extreme confusion, without some change of as great extremity?

"I mean therefore so to deal in it as I may wipe away that opinion of either uncertainty for confusion or impossibility for direction, that both the natural English may have wherein to rest, and the desirous stranger may have whereby to learn. For the performance whereof, and mine own better direction, I will first examine those means whereby other tongues of most sacred antiquity have been brought to art and form of discipline for their right writing, to the end that, by following their way, I may hit upon their right, and at the least by their precedent devise the like to theirs, where the use of our tongue and the property of our dialect will not yield flat to theirs.

"That done, I will set all the variety of our now writing, and the uncertain force of all our letters, in as much certainty as any writing can be, by these seven precepts:

"1. *General rule*, which concerneth the property and use of each letter.

"2. *Proportion*, which reduceth all words of one sound to the same writing.

"3. *Composition*, which teacheth how to write one word made of more.

"4. *Derivation*, which examineth the offspring of every original.

"5. *Distinction*, which bewrayeth the difference of sound and force in letters by some written figure or accent.

"6. *Enfranchisement*, which directeth the right writing of all incorporate foreign words.

"7. *Prerogative*, which declareth a reservation wherein common use will continue her precedence in our English writing as she hath done everywhere else, both for the form of the letter, in some places, which likes the pen better; and for the difference in writing, where some particular caveat will check a common rule.

"In all these seven I will so examine the particularities of our tongue, as either nothing shall seem strange at all, or if anything do seem, yet it shall not seem so strange but that either the self same, or the very like unto it, or the more strange than it is, shall appear to be in those things which are more familiar unto us for extraordinary learning than required of us for our ordinary use.

"And forasmuch as the eye will help many to write right by a seen precedent, which either cannot understand or cannot entend to understand the reason of a rule, therefore in the end of this treatise for right writing I purpose to set down a general table of most English words, by way of precedent, to help such plain people as cannot entend the understanding of a rule, which requireth both time and conceit in perceiving, but can easily run to a general table, which is readier to their hand. By the which table I shall also confirm the right of my rules, that they hold throughout, and by multitude of examples help some in precepts."

Thirty years later, in 1612, another teacher followed Mulcaster in advocating the study of English. This was John Brinsley, who, in *The Grammar Schoole*, writes thus :—

"There seems unto me to be a very main want in all our grammar schools generally, or in the most of them, whereof I have heard some great learned men to complain ; that there is no care had in respect to train up scholars so as they may be able to express their minds purely and readily in our own tongue, and to increase in the practice of it, as well as in the Latin and Greek; whereas our chief endeavour should be for it, and that for these reasons :

"1. Because that language which all sorts and conditions of men amongst us are to have most use of, both in speech and writing, is our own native tongue.

"2. The purity and elegance of our own language is to be esteemed a chief part of the honour of our nation, which we all ought to advance as much as in us lieth. . . .

"3. Because of those which are for a time trained up in schools, there are very few which proceed in learning, in comparison of them that follow other callings."

Among the means which he recommends "to obtain this benefit of increasing in our English tongue as in the Latin" are "continual practice of English grammatical translations," and "translating and writing English, with some other school exercises."

But, as we have seen, the study of our mother tongue continued to be generally ignored in English schools for nearly three centuries after Mulcaster and Brinsley had thus called attention to its educational value.

SCHOOL LIFE IN SHAKESPEARE'S DAY.

From Brinsley's book we get an idea of the daily life of a grammar-school boy in 1612, which probably did not differ materially from what it was in Shakespeare's boyhood.

In his chapter "Of school times, intermissions, and recreations," Brinsley says: "The school-time should begin at six: all who write Latin to make their exercises which were given overnight, in that hour before seven." To make boys punctual, "so many of them as are there at six, to have their places as they had them by election or the day before: all who come after six, every one to sit as he cometh, and so to continue that day, and until he recover his place again by the election of the form or otherwise.* If any cannot be brought by this, them to be noted in the black bill by a special mark, and feel the punishment thereof: and sometimes present correction to be used for terror;" that is, to frighten the rest.

The school work is to go on from six in the morning as follows: "Thus they are to continue until nine. . . . Then at nine to let them to have a quarter of an hour at least, or more, for intermission, either for breakfast, or else for the necessity of every one, or for honest recreation, or to prepare their exercises against the master's coming in. After, each of them to be in his place in an instant, upon the knocking of the door or some other sign, . . . so to continue until eleven of the clock, or somewhat after, to countervail the time of the inter-

---

* In a preceding chapter we are told that it was a rule for "all of a form to name who is the best of their form, and who is the best next him."

mission at nine;" that is, apparently, to make the morning session full five hours.

For the afternoon the schedule is as follows: "To be again all ready and in their places at one, in an instant; to continue until three, or half an hour after; then to have another quarter of an hour or more, as at nine, for drinking and necessities; so to continue till half an hour after five: thereby in that half hour to countervail the time at three; then to end with reading a piece of a chapter, and with singing two staves of a Psalm: lastly, with prayer to be used by the master."

These closing exercises would fill out the time until about six o'clock, making the school day nearly ten hours long, exclusive of the two intermissions at nine and three and the interval of somewhat more than an hour at noon.

It would seem that some objection had been made to the intermissions at nine and three, on the ground that the boys then "do nothing but play"; but Brinsley believed that the boys did their work the better for these brief respites from it. He adds: "It is very requisite also that they should have weekly one part of an afternoon for recreation, as a reward of diligence, obedience, and profiting; and that to be appointed at the master's discretion, either the Thursday, after the usual custom, or according to the best opportunity of the place."

The sports and recreations of the boys are to be carefully looked after. "Clownish sports, or perilous, or yet playing for money, are no way to be admitted."

Of the age at which boys went to school the same writer says: "For the time of their entrance with us,

in our country schools, it is commonly about seven or
eight years old: six is very soon. If any begin so
early, they are rather sent to the school to keep them
from troubling the house at home, and from danger,
and shrewd turns, than for any great hope and desire
their friends have that they should learn anything in
effect."

Seven, as we have seen, was the earliest age at which
boys could be admitted to the Stratford School.

SCHOOL MORALS.

Schoolboys in that olden time appear to have been
much like those nowadays. They sometimes played
truant. Jack Falstaff, in the *First Part of Henry IV.*
(ii. 4. 450) asks: "Shall the blessed sun of heaven
prove a micher and eat blackberries?" *Micher, meach-
er,* or *moocher* is now obsolete, though the practice it
suggests is not; but a contemporary dictionary of *Provincial Words and Phrases* gives this definition of the
word: "*Moocher*—a truant; a blackberry moucher.
A boy who plays truant to pick blackberries."

Idle pupils in those days often "made shift to escape correction" by methods not unlike those known
in our modern schools. Boys who had faithfully prepared their lessons would "prompt" others who had
been less diligent.

One of these fellows, named Willis, born in the same
year with Shakespeare, has recorded his youthful experience at school in a diary written later in life which
is still extant. He tells how, after being often helped
in this fashion, "it fell out on a day that one of the
eldest scholars and one of the highest form fell out

with" him "upon occasion of some boys' play abroad," and refused to "prompt" him as aforetime. He feared that he might "fall under the rod," but, gathering his wits together, managed to recite his lesson creditably; and "so" he says, "the evil intended to me by my fellow-scholar turned to my great good."

How William liked going to school we do not know, but if we are to judge from his references to schoolboys and schooldays he had little taste for it. In *As You Like It* (ii. 7. 145) we have the familiar picture of

. . . "the whining schoolboy, with his satchel
And shining morning face, creeping like snail
Unwillingly to school;"

and in *Romeo and Juliet* (ii. 1. 156) the significant similes:—

"Love goes toward love as schoolboys from their books,
But love from love, toward school with heavy looks."

Gremio, in *The Taming of the Shrew* (iii. 2. 149), when asked if he has come from the church, replies: "As willingly as e'er I came from school."

SCHOOL DISCIPLINE.

Sooth to say, the schoolmasters of that time were not likely to be remembered with much favor by their pupils in after years. There is abundant testimony to the severity of their discipline in Ascham, Peacham, and other writers of the 16th century.

8

Thomas Tusser tells of his youthful experiences at Eton in verses that have been often quoted :

" From Paul's I went, to Eton sent,
　To learn straightways the Latin phrase,
When fifty-three stripes given to me
　　At once I had ;
For fault but small or none at all
It came to pass, thus beat I was.
See, Udall, see the mercy of thee
　　To me, poor lad !"

Nicholas Udall was the master of Eton at the time.

Peacham tells of one pedagogue who used to whip his boys of a cold morning " for no other purpose than to get himself a heat." No doubt it warmed the boys too, but it is not recorded that they liked the method.

Some of the grammars of the period have on the title-page the significant woodcut of " an awful man sitting on a high chair, pointing to a book with his right hand, but with a mighty rod in his left." Lilly's Grammar, on the other hand, has the picture of a huge fruit-tree, with little boys in its branches picking the abundant fruit. I hope the urchins did not find this more suggestive of stealing apples than of gathering the rich fruit of the tree of knowledge.

Mr. Sidney Lee remarks : " A repulsive picture of the terrors which the schoolhouse had for a nervous child is drawn in a ' pretie and merry new interlude ' entitled ' The Disobedient Child, compiled by Thomas Ingeland, late student in Cambridge,' about 1560. A boy who implores his father not to force him to go to school tells of his companions' sufferings there—how

"'Their tender bodies both night and day
Are whipped and scourged, and beat like a stone,
That from top to toe the skin is away;'

and a story is repeated of how a scholar was tormented to death by 'his bloody master.' Other accounts show that the playwright has not gone far beyond the fact."

We will try to believe, however, that Master Hunt of Stratford was of a milder disposition. Holofernes seems well disposed towards his pupils, and is invited to dine with the father of one of them; and Sir Hugh Evans, in his examination of William Page, has a very kindly manner. It is to be noted, indeed, that in few of Shakespeare's references to school life is there any mention of whipping as a punishment.

Roger Ascham, in his *Scholemaster*, advocated gentler discipline than was usual in the schools of his day. His book, indeed, owed its origin to his interest in this matter.

In 1563, Ascham, who was then Latin Secretary to Queen Elizabeth, was dining with Sir William Cecil (afterwards Lord Burleigh), when the conversation turned to the subject of education, from news of the running away of some boys from Eton, where there was much beating. Ascham argued that young children were sooner allured by love than driven by beating to obtain good learning. Sir Richard Sackville, father of Thomas Sackville, said nothing at the dinner-table, but he afterwards drew Ascham aside, agreed with his opinions, lamented his own past loss by a harsh school-master, and said, Ascham tells us in the preface to his book: "'Seeing it is but in vain to lament things past, and also wisdom to look to things to come, surely, God willing, if God lend me life, I will make this my mishap some occasion of good hap to little Robert Sackville, my son's son. For whose bringing up I would gladly, if it so please you, use specially your good advice. I hear say you have a son much of his age [Ascham had three little sons]; we will deal thus together. Point you out a schoolmaster who by your order shall teach my son's son and yours, and for all the rest I will provide, yea, though they three do cost me a couple of hundred pounds by year; and besides you shall find me as fast a friend to you and yours as perchance any you have.' Which promise the worthy gentleman surely kept with me until his dying day." The conversation ended with a request that Ascham would "put in some order of writing the chief points of this our talk, concerning the right order of teaching and honesty of living, for the good bringing up of children and young men."

Ascham accordingly wrote *The Scholemaster*, which was published in 1570 (two years after his death) by his widow, with a dedication to Sir William Cecil.

In the very first page of the book, Ascham, referring to training in "the making of Latins," or writing the language, says: "For the scholar is commonly beat for the making, when the master were more worthy to be beat for the mending or rather marring of the same; the master many times being as ignorant as the child what to say properly and fitly to the matter."

Again he says: "I do gladly agree with all good schoolmasters in these points: to have children brought to good perfectness in learning; to all honesty in manners; to have all faults rightly amended; to have every vice severely corrected; but for the order and way that leadeth rightly to these points we somewhat differ.

For commonly, many schoolmasters — some, as I have seen, more, as I have heard tell—be of so crooked a nature, as, when they meet with a hard-witted scholar, they rather break him than bow him, rather mar him than mend him. For when the schoolmaster is angry with some other matter, then will he soonest fall to beat his scholar; and though he himself should be punished for his folly, yet must he beat some scholar for his pleasure, though there be no cause for him to do so, nor yet fault in the scholar to deserve so. These, you will say, be fond [that is, foolish] school-masters, and few they be that be found to be such. They be fond, indeed, but surely over many such be found everywhere. But this will I say, that even the wisest of your great beaters do as oft punish nature as they do correct faults. Yea, many times the better nature is sorely punished; for, if one, by quickness of wit, take his lesson readily, another, by hardness of wit, taketh it not so speedily, the first is always commended, the other is commonly punished; when a wise school-master should rather discreetly consider the right dis-position of both their natures, and not so much weigh what either of them is able to do now, as what either of them is likely to do hereafter. For this I know, not only by reading of books in my study, but also by experience of life abroad in the world, that those which be commonly the wisest, the best learned, and best men also, when they be old, were never com-monly the quickest of wit when they were young."

The result of ordinary school training, with the free use of the rod, as Ascham says, is that boys "carry commonly from the school with them a perpetual hatred of their master and a continual contempt for learning." He adds: "If ten gentlemen be asked why they forget so soon in court that which they were learning so long in school, eight of them, or let me be blamed, will lay the fault on their ill handling by their schoolmasters." The sum of the matter is that "learning should be taught rather by love than fear," and "the schoolhouse should be counted a sanctuary against fear.

But Ascham, like Mulcaster and Brinsley, was far in advance of his age, and it is doubtful whether his wise counsel with regard to methods of discipline met with any greater favor among teachers than theirs concerning the importance of the study of English.

WHEN WILLIAM LEFT SCHOOL.

How long William remained in the Grammar School we do not know, but probably not more than six years, or until he was thirteen. In 1577 his father was beginning to have bad luck in his business, and the boy very likely had to be taken from school for work of some sort.

As Ben Jonson says, Shakespeare had "small Latin and less Greek"—perhaps none—and this was probably due to his leaving the Grammar School before the average age. However that may have been, we may be pretty sure that all the regular schooling he ever had was got there.

Part IV
GAMES AND SPORTS

BOYISH GAMES

YOUNG William may have found life at the Henley Street house and at the Grammar School rather dull, but there was no lack of diversion and recreation out of doors. Household comforts and attractions were meagre enough in those days, but holidays were frequent, and rural sports and pastimes for young and old were many and varied. We may be sure that Shakespeare enjoyed these to the full. His writings abound in allusions to them which were doubtless reminiscences of his own boyhood.

Many of the children's games to which he refers are

familiar to small folk now, especially in the rural districts. Hide-and-seek, for example—also known as "hoop-and-hide" and "harry-racket"—is probably the play that Hamlet had in mind when he exclaimed (iv. 2. 33), "Hide, fox, and after." Blind-man's-buff is also alluded to by Hamlet when, chiding his mother for preferring his uncle to his father, he asks:

> "What devil was 't
> That thus hath cozen'd you at hoodman-blind."

A dictionary of Shakespeare's time couples this name for the pastime with the one that has survived: "The Hoodwinke play, or hoodmanblinde, in some places called the blindmanbuf." Hamlet's question is evidently suggested by the practice of making the "blind man" guess whom he has caught—as Greek and Roman boys did when they played the game.

In the grave-digging scene (v. 1. 100) Hamlet asks: "Did these bones cost no more the breeding but to play at loggats with them?" This refers to the throwing of *loggats* or *loggets*—small logs, or sticks of wood much like "Indian clubs"—at a stake, the player coming nearest to it being the winner.

In a poem of 1611 we find loggats in a list of games with sundry others that are still in vogue:—

> "To wrastle, play at stooleball, or to runne,
> To pich the Barre, or to shoote off a Gunne,
> To play at Loggets, Nine-holes, or Ten-pinnes;
> To try it out at Foot-ball by the shinnes."

Stool-ball, commonly played by girls and women, sometimes in company with boys or men, is to this day a village pastime in some parts of England. It is essentially a lighter kind of cricket, but is more ancient than that game.

Pitching the bar was an athletic exercise still common in Scotland. Scott alludes to it in *The Lady of the Lake*, iv. 559 :—

> "Now, if thou strik'st her but one blow,
> I'll pitch thee from the cliff as far
> As ever peasant pitch'd a bar!"

And again, in the account of the sports at Stirling Castle, v. 647 :—

> "Their arms the brawny yeomen bare
> To hurl the massive bar in air."

A poet of the 16th century tells us that to throw "the stone, the bar, or the plummet" is a commendable exercise for kings and princes ; and, according to the old chroniclers, it was a favorite diversion with Henry VIII. after his accession to the throne.

Nine-holes, a game in which nine holes were made in a board or in the ground at which small balls were rolled, is among the rustic sports enumerated by Drayton in the *Poly-Olbion.*

There were many ball-games besides stool-ball in the days of Elizabeth, from the simple hand-ball, which Homer represents the princess of Corcyra as playing with her maidens, to more complicated exercises, among which we can recognize the germ of the later "rounders," out of which our Yankee base-ball has been developed.

The term *base*, as denoting a starting-point or goal, occurs in the name of other than ball-games, especially in "prisoners' base"—sometimes "prisoners' bars," or "prison-bars"—which was popular long before Shakespeare was born. It is played by two sides, who occupy opposite bases, or "homes." Any player running out from his base is chased by the opposite party, and if caught is made a prisoner. It belongs to a class of old games, one of the most popular of which was called "barley-break."

Originally, this was played by three couples, male and female; one couple was stationed in "hell" or the space between the two goals, and tried to catch the others as they ran across. It is thus described by Sir Philip Sidney in the *Arcadia* :—

"Then couples three be straight allotted there;
    They of both ends the middle two do fly;
The two that in mid-space, Hell called, were
    Must strive, with waiting foot and watching eye,
To catch of them, and them to Hell to bear,
    That they, as well as they, may Hell supply."

Later it came to be played by any number of young people, of either sex or both, with one person in "hell" at the start. The game was kept up until all had been captured and brought into this Inferno. In this form, under the name of "Lill-lill"—which was the signal cry of the person between the goals for beginning the sport—it was played by schoolboys in eastern Massachusetts fifty years ago.

Barley-break is often alluded to by the dramatists and lyrists of Shakespeare's day, and complete poems were written upon it by Suckling, Herrick, and others. Shakespeare does not mention it, though he has several references to prisoners' base; as in *Cymbeline* (v. 3. 20) :—

> " lads more like to run
> The country base than to commit such slaughter."

To "bid a base," or "the base," was a common phrase for challenging to a game of this kind, and we often find it used figuratively; as in *Venus and Adonis*, 303, in the spirited description of the horse, which, like many other passages, shows Shakespeare's interest in the animal :—

> "Sometimes he scuds far off, and there he stares;
>   Anon he starts at stirring of a feather;
> To bid the wind a base he now prepares,
>   And whether he run or fly they know not whether,
> For through his mane and tail the high wind sings,
> Fanning the hairs, who wave like feather'd wings."

In the *Two Gentlemen of Verona* (i. 2. 97), Lucetta says to Julia, with a pun upon the phrase: " Indeed, I bid the base for Proteus."

Drayton, in the *Poly-Olbion*, includes this game with others that have been described above : " At hood-wink, barley-brake, at tick [that is, tag], or prison-base "; and Spenser in the *Shepherd's Calendar* (October) refers to it among rustic pastimes: " In rymes, in ridles, and in bydding base."

Foot-ball is mentioned by Shakespeare in the *Comedy of Errors* (ii. 1. 82), where Dromio of Ephesus says to his mistress Adriana, who has been chiding him :—

"Am I so round with you as you with me,
   That like a foot-ball you do spurn me thus?
   You spurn me hence, and he will spurn me hither;
   If I last in this service, you must case me in leather."

In *Lear* (i. 4. 95), Oswald says to Kent, "I'll not be
struck, my lord!" and Kent replies, "Nor tripped neither,
you base foot-ball player."

The game was popular with the common people of
England at least as early as the reign of Edward III.,
for in 1349 it was prohibited by royal edict—not, apparently, from any particular objection to the game in itself, but because it was believed to interfere with the
popular interest in archery.

The sport was, however, a rough one then as now.
Alexander Barclay, who died in 1552, in one of his
Eclogues, tells how

"The sturdie plowman, lustie, strong, and bold,
   Overcometh the winter, with driving the foote-ball,
   Forgetting labour and many a grievous fall."

Edmund Waller, in the next century, writes:—

"As when a sort [company] of lusty shepherds try
   Their force at foot-ball; care of victory
   Makes them salute so rudely breast to breast,
   That their encounter seems too rough for jest."

King James I., in his *Basilicon*—a set of rules for the
nurture and conduct of Henry, Prince of Wales, the
heir-apparent to the throne—says:—
   "Certainly bodily exercises and games are very commendable, as well for ban'shing of idleness, the mother

of all vice, as for making the body able and durable for travell, which is very necessarie for a king. But from this court I debarre all rough and violent exercises; as the foote-ball, meeter for lameing than making able the users thereof; likewise such tumbling tricks as only serve for comedians and balladines [theatrical dancers] to win their bread with; but the exercises that I would have you to use, although but moderately, not making a craft of them, are, running, leaping, wrestling, fencing, dancing, and playing at the caitch, or tenise, archery, palle-malle, and such like other fair and pleasant field-games."

Burton, in his *Anatomy of Melancholy*, published in 1621, mentions foot-ball among the "common recreations of country folks," as distinguished from the "disports of greater men," or those higher in rank.

In *Romeo and Juliet* (i. 4. 41) Mercutio says to Romeo, "If thou art Dun, we'll draw thee from the mire"—that is, of love. This is an allusion to a rural game which seems to have been a favorite for several centuries, and to which scores of references, literal and figurative, are to be found in writers of all classes.

In Chaucer's *Canterbury Tales* (16936) we read:—

"Ther gan our hoste for to jape and play,
And sayde, 'sires, what? Dun is in the myre;'"

Bishop Butler, more than three hundred years later, writes: "they mean to leave reformation, like Dun in the mire."

Gifford, in his notes on Ben Jonson's *Masque of Christmas*, tells us (in 1816) that he himself had "often played at this game." He describes it substantially as

follows : A log of wood called "Dun the cart-horse"
is brought into the middle of the room, and some one
cries, "Dun is stuck in the mire." Two of the players
try, with or without ropes, to drag it out, but, pretending to be unable to do so, call for help. Others come
forward, and make awkward attempts to draw out the
log, which they manage, if possible, to drop upon a
companion's toes, causing "much honest mirth."

It is remarkable that so simple a diversion could have
been popular with generation after generation of British
young folk, and that they should apparently recall it
with so much interest in later years. Verily, our forefathers in the old country were easily amused.

In *Antony and Cleopatra* (iii. 13. 91) we find an allusion to another game equally simple—if, indeed, it be
not too simple to be called a game. Antony says :—

"Authority melts from me; of late, when I cried 'Ho !'
  Like boys unto a muss, kings would start forth
  And cry 'Your will?'"

A "muss" was merely a scramble for small coins or
other things thrown down to be taken by those who
could seize them. Ben Jonson, in *The Magnetic Lady*
(iv. 1), says :—

"The moneys rattle not, nor are they thrown
  To make a muss yet 'mong the gamesome suitors";

In the same author's *Bartholomew Fair* (iv. 1), when
the costard-monger's basket of pears is overturned,
Cokes begins to scramble for them, crying, "Ods so ! a
muss, a muss, a muss, a muss !"

Dryden, in the prologue to *Widow Ranter*, says :—

> "Bauble and cap no sooner are thrown down
> But there's a muss of more than half the town."

This is the origin of the modern colloquial or slang use of *muss*.

"Handy-dandy" was a childish play in which something was shaken between the two hands, and a guess made as to the hand in which it remained. It is alluded to in *Lear* (iv. 6. 157) : "See how yond justice rails upon yond simple thief. Hark, in thine ear: change places; and, handy-dandy, which is the justice, which is the thief?" The game is very ancient, being mentioned by Aristotle, Plato, and other Greek writers.

In the *Midsummer - Night's Dream* (ii. 2. 98) Titania, lamenting the results of the quarrel with Oberon, says :—

> "The nine men's morris is fill'd up with mud,
> And the quaint mazes in the wanton green
> For lack of tread are undistinguishable."

The "nine men's morris" was a Warwickshire game which is still kept up among the rural population of the county. It is played on three squares, one within another, with lines uniting the angles and the middle of the sides; the opponents having each nine "men," which are moved somewhat as in draughts, or checkers.

In the country the squares were often cut in the green turf, the sides of the outer one being sometimes three or four yards long. In towns, they were chalked upon the pavement. It was also played indoors upon a board.

9

A woodcut of 1520 represents two monkeys engaged at it. It was sometimes called "nine men's merrils,"

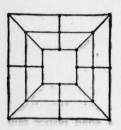

"MORRIS" BOARD

from *merelles*, the old French name for the "men," or counters, with which it was played.

The "quaint mazes" in Titania's speech, according to the best English critics, refer to a game known as "running the figure of eight."

Space would fail to describe other boyish games of the time, even those mentioned in the writings of Shakespeare ; and I need not say anything of leap-frog, trundling-hoop, battledore and shuttlecock, seesaw — sometimes called "riding the wild mare" — tops, and many other pastimes in perennial favor with boys.

Mulcaster, the head-master of Merchant-Taylors School in London (see page 106 above), in a book printed in 1581, enumerates as suitable exercises for boys : "indoors, dancing, wrestling, fencing, the top and scourge [whip-top]; outdoor, walking, running, leaping, swimming, riding, hunting, shooting, and playing at the ball — hand-ball, tennis, foot-ball, arm-ball." William doubtless had experience in most of these, swimming in the Avon among them.

SWIMMING AND FISHING.

The spirited description of Ferdinand swimming (*The Tempest*, ii. 1. 113–121) could have been written only by one well skilled in the art :—

"I saw him beat the surges under him,
And ride upon their backs; he trod the water,
Whose enmity he flung aside, and breasted
The surge most swoln that met him; his bold head
'Bove the contentious waves he kept, and oar'd
Himself with his good arms in lusty stroke
To the shore, that o'er his wave-worn basis bow'd,
As stooping to relieve him. I not doubt
He came alive to land."

There are many other allusions to swimming in the plays which indicate the writer's personal acquaintance with the exercise; as in *Macbeth*, i. 2. 8 :—

"As two spent swimmers that do cling together
And choke their art."

The swimming match between Cæsar and Cassius (*Julius Cæsar*, i. 2. 100) is described with sympathetic vigor. Cassius says to Brutus :—

"We can both
Endure the winter's cold as well as he.
For once, upon a raw and gusty day,
The troubled Tiber chafing with her shores,
Cæsar said to me, 'Dar'st thou, Cassius, now
Leap in with me into this angry flood,
And swim to yonder point?' Upon the word,
Accoutred as I was, I plunged in,
And bade him follow; so, indeed, he did.
The torrent roar'd, and we did buffet it
With lusty sinews, throwing it aside
And stemming it with hearts of controversy.
But ere we could arrive the point propos'd,
Cæsar cried, 'Help me, Cassius, or I sink!'
I, as Æneas, our great ancestor,

Did from the flames of Troy upon his shoulder
The old Anchises bear, so from the waves of Tiber
Did I the tired Cæsar."

Of course William often went a-fishing in the Avon,
and understood, as Ursula says in *Much Ado About
Nothing* (iii. 1. 26), that

" The pleasant'st angling is to see the fish
   Cut with her golden oars the silver stream,
   And greedily devour the treacherous bait."

BEAR-BAITING.

The boy must often have seen a bear-baiting, for the
cruel sport was popular with all classes, from sovereign
to peasant. Queen Elizabeth was fond of it, as was
her sister Mary; and it was one of the "princely pleasures" provided for the entertainment of the former at
Kenilworth in 1575, when thirteen great bears were
worried by bandogs.

On another occasion, when Elizabeth gave a splendid dinner to the French ambassadors, she entertained
them afterwards with the baiting of bulls and bears;
and she herself watched the sport till six at night.
The next day the ambassadors went to see another
exhibition of the same kind. A Danish ambassador,
some years later, was entertained by the Queen at
Greenwich with a bear-baiting and "other merry disports," as the chronicle expresses it.

Elizabeth was a lover of the drama, but was unwill-
ing that it should interfere with these brute tragedies.
In 1591, a royal edict forbade plays to be acted on

Thursdays, because bear-baiting and similar sports had usually been practised on that day. This order was followed by one to the same effect from the lord mayor, who complained that "in divers places the players do use to recite their plays to the great hurt and

THE BEAR GARDEN, LONDON

destruction of the game of bear-baiting and such like pastimes, which are maintained for her majesty's pleasure."

The clergy were as fond of these amusements as

their parishioners appear to have been.   Thomas Cart-
wright, in a book published in 1572, says : " If there
be a bear or a bull to be baited in the afternoon, or a
jackanapes to ride on horseback, the minister hurries
the service over in a shameful manner, in order to be
present at the show."

It is on record that at a certain place in Cheshire, "the town bear having died, the corporation in
1601 gave orders to *sell their Bible* in order to purchase another."   At another place, when a bear was
wanted for baiting at a town festival, the churchwardens pawned the Bible from the sacred desk in
order to obtain the means of enjoying their immemo-
rial sport.

There are many allusions to bear-baiting in Shakespeare.   In *Twelfth Night* (i. 3. 98) Sir Andrew Ague-
cheek says : " I would I had bestowed that time in the
tongues [that is, the study of languages] that I have in
fencing, dancing, and bear-baiting : O, had I but followed the arts !"   In the same play (ii. 5. 9) Fabian,
referring to Malvolio, says to Sir Toby, " You know, he
brought me out of favor with my lady about a bear-
baiting here"; and Fabian replies, "To anger him
we'll have the bear back again."   There is a figurative
reference to the sport in this play (iii. 1. 130) where
Olivia says to the disguised Viola :—

> " Have you not set mine honour at the stake,
>   And baited it with all the unmuzzled thoughts
>   That tyrannous heart can think ?"

In 2 *Henry VI.* (v. 1. 148) we find a similar figure
where York says to Clifford :—

> " Call hither to the stake my two brave bears,
>   That with the very shaking of their chains
>   They may astonish these fell-lurking curs:
>   Bid Salisbury and Warwick come to me."

The amusing dialogue between Slender and Anne
Page, in the *Merry Wives of Windsor* (i. i. 307), may
be added :—

> " *Slender.* Why do your dogs bark so? be there bears i'
> the town?
>   *Anne.* I think there are, sir, I heard them talked of.
>   *Slender.* I love the sport well; but I shall as soon quar-
> rel at it as any man in England.—You are afraid, if you
> see the bear loose, are you not?
>   *Anne.* Ay, indeed, sir.
>   *Slender.* That's meat and drink to me, now: I have
> seen Sackerson loose twenty times, and have taken him
> by the chain; but, I warrant you, the women have so
> cried and shriek'd at it, that it passed [passed descrip-
> tion]; but women, indeed, cannot abide 'em; they are
> very ill-favoured rough things."

Sackerson was a famous bear exhibited at Paris Garden, a popular bear-garden on the Bankside in London, near the Globe Theatre. An old epigram refers
to the place and the animal thus :—

> " Publius, a student of the common law,
>   To Paris-garden doth himself withdraw,
>   Leaving old Ployden, Dyer, and Broke alone,
>   To see old Harry Hunkes and Sacarson ;"

that is, neglecting Ployden and other writers on law
for the sports at the bear-garden.

For the bear to get loose was a serious matter. We

read in a diary of 1554 that at a bear-baiting on the Bankside "the great blind bear broke loose, and in running away he caught a servingman by the calf of the leg and bit a great piece away," so that "within three days after he died."

James I. prohibited baiting on Sundays, but did not otherwise discourage it. In the time of the Commonwealth Paris Garden was shut up, the bear was killed, and the amusement forbidden; but with the Restoration it was revived, and continued to be popular until the early part of the next century. In 1802 an attempt was made in Parliament to suppress it altogether, but the House of Commons by a majority of thirteen refused to pass the bill. It was not until the year 1835 that baiting was finally abolished by an act of Parliament, forbidding "the keeping of any house, pit, or other place, for baiting or fighting any bull, bear, dog, or other animal."

COCK-FIGHTING AND COCK-THROWING.

Cock-fighting was another barbarous amusement that was very early in great favor in England. Fitzstephen, who died in 1191, records that in London "every year at Shrove Tuesday the schoolboys do bring cocks to their master, and all the forenoon they delight themselves in cock-fighting"; and it is not until the 16th century that we find Dean Colet, the founder of St. Paul's School, objecting to it as an amusement for the pupils.

The good lady who founded the Nottingham grammar school in 1513 was content with restricting the sport to "twice a year."

In Scotland cock-fights were sanctioned as a school recreation till the middle of the last century, and the master received a fee, called "cock-penny," from the boys on the occasion. As late as 1790, at Applecross, in Ross-shire, "the cock-fight dues" were reckoned as a part of the schoolmaster's income.

Shakespeare has only two or three allusions to cock-fighting in his works. Antony says of Octavius (*Antony and Cleopatra*, ii. 3. 36) :—

> "His cocks do win the battle still of mine,
>   When it is all to nought; and his quails ever
>   Beat mine, inhoop'd, at odds."

Dr. Johnson, in a note on the passage, says : "The ancients used to match quails as we match cocks." The birds were *inhooped*, or confined within a circle, to keep them "up to the scratch"; or, according to some authorities, the one that was driven out of the hoop was considered beaten.

Hamlet, when at the point of death, exclaims :—

> "O, I die, Horatio;
> The potent poison quite o'er-crows my spirit!"

He means that the poison triumphs over him, as a victorious cock over his beaten antagonist.

In the *Taming of the Shrew* (ii. 1. 228), Katharina says to Petruchio, "You crow too like a craven." This word *craven*, which meant a base coward, was often applied to a vanquished knight who had not fought bravely, and hence came to be used with reference to a beaten or cowardly cock, as it is in this passage.

Another popular diversion, especially among the

boys, was "throwing at cocks," in which the bird was tied to a stake and sticks thrown at it until it was killed. This sport, which dates back to the 14th century, and which was not uncommon in England less than a hundred years ago, is said to have been peculiar to that country.

Sir Thomas More, writing in the 16th century, tells of his own skill in his childhood in casting a "cock-stele," that is, a stick or cudgel to throw at a cock. The amusement was regularly practised on Shrove Tuesday.

In some places the cock was put into an earthen vessel made for the purpose, with only his head and tail exposed to view. The vessel was then suspended across the street twelve or fourteen feet from the ground, to be thrown at. The boy who broke the pot and freed the cock from his confinement had him for a reward.

According to a popular superstition of Shakespeare's day, the cock was supposed to be a kind of devil's messenger, from his crowing after Peter's denial of his Master. Clergymen sometimes made this an excuse for their enjoyment in cock-throwing.

Shakespeare makes no reference to this vulgar prejudice against the cock. On the contrary, in a very beautiful passage in *Hamlet* (i. 1. 158), he associates the bird with the joy and hope of Christmas:—

" Some say that ever 'gainst that season comes
  Wherein our Saviour's birth is celebrated,
  The bird of dawning singeth all night long;
  And then, they say, no spirit can walk abroad,
  The nights are wholesome, then no planets strike,
  No fairy takes, nor witch hath power to charm,
  So hallow'd and so gracious is the time."

OTHER CRUEL SPORTS.

When the Chief Justice says to Falstaff (2 *Henry IV.* i. 2. 255), " Fare you well ; commend me to my cousin Westmoreland," the fat knight mutters, " If I do, fillip me with a three-man beetle." The allusion is to a cruel sport which is said to have been common with Warwickshire boys. A toad was put on one end of a short board placed across a small log, and the other end was then struck with a bat, thus throwing the creature high in the air. This was called *filliping* the toad. A *three-man beetle* was a heavy rammer with three handles used in driving piles, requiring three men to wield it. Such a beetle would evidently be needed for filliping a weight like Falstaff's.

Falstaff alludes to another piece of boyish cruelty to animals in *The Merry Wives of Windsor* (v. 1. 26) when he says, after the cudgelling he has received from Ford, " Since I plucked geese, played truant, and whipped top, I knew not what 'twas to be beaten till lately." The young barbarians of Shakespeare's time thought it fine sport to pull the feathers from a live goose. If they sometimes got whipped for it, we may suppose that it was solely for the mischief done to private property. When their elders were fond of bear-baiting, cock-fighting, and other brutal amusements, the boys would hardly be punished for torturing a domestic animal unless its value was lessened by the ill-treatment.

Whether Shakespeare in his boyhood was guilty of thoughtless cruelty like this, as boys are apt to be even nowadays, we cannot say ; but later in life he recognized its wantonness, and more than once reproved

the brutality of children of larger growth in their sports
and amusements.

In *Lear* (iv. 1. 38) Gloster says bitterly :—

> " As flies to wanton boys are we to the gods,
>   They kill us for their sport."

In the same play (iv. 7. 36) Cordelia, referring to the
unnatural conduct of Goneril in turning her old father
out of doors in the storm, exclaims :—

> "Mine enemy's dog,
> Though he had bit me, should have stood that night
> Against my fire !"

The poet did not forget that even an insect may
suffer pain. In *Measure for Measure* (iii. 1. 79) Isabella
says to her brother :—

> " Darest thou die ?
> The sense of death is most in apprehension ;
> And the poor beetle, that we tread upon,
> In corporal sufferance finds a pang as great
> As when a giant dies."

In *As You Like It* (ii 1. 21) the banished Duke in
the Forest of Arden laments the necessity of killing
deer for food :—

> " *Duke S.* Come, shall we go and kill us venison ?
> And yet it irks me, the poor dappled fools,
> Being native burghers of this desert city,
> Should in their own confines with forked heads
> Have their round haunches gor'd.

1 *Lord.*   Indeed, my lord,
The melancholy Jaques grieves at that,
And, in that kind, swears you do more usurp
Than doth your brother that hath banish'd you.
To-day my lord of Amiens and myself
Did steal behind him as he lay along
Under an oak, whose antique root peeps out
Upon the brook that brawls along this wood:
To the which place a poor sequester'd stag,
That from the hunters' aim had ta'en a hurt,
Did come to languish; and, indeed, my lord,
The wretched animal heav'd forth such groans,
That their discharge did stretch his leathern coat
Almost to bursting, and the big round tears
Cours'd one another down his innocent nose
In piteous chase: and thus the hairy fool,
Much marked of the melancholy Jaques,
Stood on the extremest verge of the swift brook,
Augmenting it with tears."

The sympathy of the Duke and the First Lord for
the "poor dappled fools" is sincere, but that of Jaques,
as we understand when we come to know him better,
is mere sentimental affectation. We may be sure that
the Duke rather than Jaques represents the feeling of
Shakespeare himself for the unfortunate creatures.

In another part of the same play (i. 2) the poet,
through the mouth of Touchstone, the philosophic
Fool, gives a sly rap at people who find amusement in
brutal games. Le Beau, a courtier who is really a kind-
hearted fellow, as his conduct elsewhere proves, meeting Rosalind and Celia, tells them that they have just
"lost much fine sport," that is, as he explains, some
"good wrestling." They ask him to "tell the manner
of it," and he says:—

"There comes an old man and his three sons,—three proper young men of excellent growth and presence. The eldest of the three wrestled with Charles, the duke's wrestler; which Charles in a moment threw him, and broke three of his ribs, that there is little hope of life in him : so he served the second, and so the third. Yonder they lie ; the poor old man, their father, making such pitiful dole over them that all the beholders take his part with weeping.

Rosalind. Alas!

Touchstone. But what is the sport, monsieur, that the ladies have lost?

Le Beau. Why, this that I speak of.

Touchstone. Thus men may grow wiser every day! It is the first time that ever I heard breaking of ribs was sport for ladies.

Celia. Or I, I promise thee."

Wrestling, by the bye, was a common exercise with the rural youth in the time of Elizabeth, and no doubt the smaller boys often tried their hand at it.

ARCHERY.

Archery was a popular pastime in those days with young and old. The bow and arrow continued to be used in warfare long after the discovery of gunpowder. As late as 1572 Queen Elizabeth promised to furnish six thousand men for Charles IX. of France, half of whom were to be archers. Ralph Smithe, a writer on Martial Discipline in the reign of the same queen, says : "Captains and officers should be skilful of that most noble weapon the long bow; and to see that their soldiers, according to their draught and strength, have good bows," etc. In the reign of Henry VIII. several laws were made for promoting the use of the long bow. One of these required every male subject to exercise himself in archery, and also to keep a long bow with arrows continually in his house. Men sixty years old, ecclesiastics, and certain justices were exempted from this obligation. Fathers and guardians were commanded to teach the male children the use of the long bow, and to have bows provided for them as soon as they were seven years old; and masters were ordered to furnish bows for their apprentices, and to compel them to learn to shoot therewith upon holidays and at every other convenient time.

In 1545 Roger Ascham published his *Toxophilus, or the Schole of Shooting*, in which he advocated the practice of archery among scholars as among the people at large, and gave full directions for making and using bows and arrows. He dedicated the book to Henry VIII., who rewarded the patriotic service with a pension of ten pounds a year.

Ascham urged that attention should be paid to training the young in archery; "for children," he said, "if sufficient pains are taken with them at the outset, may much more easily be taught to shoot well than men," because the latter have frequently more trouble to unlearn their bad habits than would suffice to teach them good ones.

One of the statutes of Henry VIII. forbade any person who had reached the age of twenty-four years from shooting at a mark less than 220 yards distant; and a writer of 1602 tells of Cornish archers who could send an arrow to a distance of 480 yards. Matches of archery were held under the patronage of Henry VIII. and Elizabeth, to encourage skill in the art. At one of these, held in London in 1583, there was a procession of three thousand archers, each of whom had a long bow and four arrows. Nine hundred and forty-two of the men had chains of gold about their necks. The company was guarded by four thousand whifflers (heralds or ushers) and billmen, besides pages and footmen. They went through the city to Smithfield, where, after performing various evolutions, they "shot at a target for honor."

There are many allusions to archery in Shakespeare's works, only one or two of which can be mentioned here. In 2 *Henry IV.* (iii. 2. 49) Shallow, referring to " old Double," who is dead, says of him: " Jesu, Jesu, dead ! a' drew a good bow ; and dead ! a' shot a fine shoot : John o' Gaunt loved him well, and betted much money on his head. Dead ! a' would have clapped i' the clout at twelve score ; and carried you a forehand shaft at fourteen and fourteen and a half, that it would have done a man's heart good to see."

To "clap in the clout" was to hit the *clout*, or the white mark in the centre of the target. " Twelve score " means twelve score or two hundred and forty *yards;* and the "fourteen" and "fourteen and a half " also refer to scores of yards. The "forehand shaft" is among the kinds of arrow mentioned by Ascham, who says: "the forehand must have a big breast, to bear the great might of the bow "; that is, the great strain in shooting at long range.

In *Much Ado About Nothing* (i. 1. 39) Beatrice, making fun of Benedick, says: " He set up his bills here in Messina and challenged Cupid at the flight ; and my uncle's fool, reading the challenge, subscribed for Cupid, and challenged him at the bird-bolt"; that is, he posted a challenge, inviting Cupid to compete with him in shooting with the *flight*, a kind of light-feathered arrow used for great distances. The fool subscribed (wrote underneath) a challenge to Benedick to try his skill with the cross-bow and *bird-bolt*, a short, thick, blunt-headed arrow used by children and fools, who could not be trusted with pointed arrows. The point of the joke is that Benedick, though he has the vanity to think he can compete in feats of archery with an expert bowman like Cupid, is only fit to contend with beginners and blunderers.

In *Love's Labour's Lost* (iv. 3. 23) Cupid's own arrow is jocosely called a bird-bolt. Biron, finding that the King has fallen in love with the French Princess, exclaims, " Shot, by heaven ! Proceed, sweet Cupid ; thou hast thumped him with thy bird-bolt."

HUNTING

Professor Baynes, in his article on Shakespeare in the *Encyclopædia Britannica*, says : " It is clear that in his early years the poet had some experience of hunting, hawking, coursing, wild-duck shooting, and the like. Many of these sports were pursued by the local gentry and the yeomen together ; and the poet, as the son of a well-connected burgess of Stratford, who had recently been mayor of the town and possessed estates in the county, would be well entitled to share in them, while his handsome presence and courteous bearing would be likely to ensure him a hearty welcome."

His love for dogs and horses is illustrated by many passages in his works. There was never a more graphic description of hounds than he puts into the mouth of Theseus in the *Midsummer-Night's Dream* (iv. 1. 108):—

"*Theseus.* Go, one of you, find out the forester;
For now our observation is perform'd:
And since we have the vaward of the day,
My love shall hear the music of my hounds.
Uncouple in the western valley; let them go!—
Despatch, I say, and find the forester.—
We will, fair queen, up to the mountain's top,
And mark the musical confusion
Of hounds and echo in conjunction.
    Hippolyta. I was with Hercules and Cadmus once,
When in a wood of Crete they bay'd the bear
With hounds of Sparta: never did I hear
Such gallant chiding: for, besides the groves,
The skies, the fountains, every region near
Seem'd all one mutual cry. I never heard
So musical a discord, such sweet thunder.
    Theseus. My hounds are bred out of the Spartan kind,
So flew'd, so sanded, and their heads are hung
With ears that sweep away the morning dew;
Crook-knee'd, and dew-lapp'd like Thessalian bulls;
Slow in pursuit, but match'd in mouth like bells,
Each under each. A cry more tuneable
Was never holla'd to, nor cheer'd with horn,
In Crete, in Sparta, nor in Thessaly:
Judge when you hear."

The talk of the hunters about the dogs in *The Taming of the Shrew* (ind. 1. 16) is in the same vein:—

"*Lord.* Huntsman, I charge thee, tender well my hounds—
Brach Merriman, the poor cur, is emboss'd—
And couple Clowder with the deep-mouth'd brach.
Saw'st thou not, boy, how Silver made it good

GARDEN AT NEW PLACE

At the hedge corner, in the coldest fault?
I would not lose the dog for twenty pound.

 1 *Hunter.* Why, Bellman is as good as he, my lord;
He cried upon it at the merest loss,
And twice to-day pick'd out the dullest scent:
Trust me, I take him for the better dog.

 Lord. Thou art a fool: if Echo were as fleet,
I would esteem him worth a dozen such.
But sup them well, and look unto them all;
To-morrow I intend to hunt again."

In the *Merry Wives of Windsor* (i. 1. 96) Page de-
fends his greyhound against the criticisms of Slender,
and Shallow takes his part :—

 "*Slender.* How does your fallow greyhound, sir? I
heard say, he was outrun on Cotsall.

 Page. It could not be judged, sir.

 Slender. You'll not confess, you'll not confess.

 Shallow. That he will not.—'T is your fault, 't is your
fault: 't is a good dog.

 Page. A cur, sir.

 Shallow. Sir, he 's a good dog, and a fair dog; can there
be more said? he is good and fair."

Cotsall (or *Cotswold*) is an allusion to the Cotswold
downs in Gloucestershire, celebrated for coursing (hunting the hare), for which their fine turf fitted them, and
also for other rural sports.

The description of the horse in *Venus and Adonis*
(259), a youthful work of Shakespeare's, is famous :—

"But, lo, from forth a copse that neighbours by,
 A breeding jennet, lusty, young, and proud,
Adonis' trampling courser doth espy,
 And forth she rushes, snorts, and neighs aloud;

The strong-neck'd steed, being tied unto a tree,
Breaketh his rein, and to her straight goes he.

Imperiously he leaps, he neighs, he bounds,
And now his woven girths he breaks asunder;
The bearing earth with his hard hoof he wounds,
Whose hollow womb resounds like heaven's thunder:
    The iron bit he crushes 'tween his teeth,
    Controlling what he was controlled with.

His ears up-prick'd; his braided hanging mane
Upon his compass'd crest now stand on end;
His nostrils drink the air, and forth again,
As from a furnace, vapours doth he send;
    His eye, which scornfully glisters like fire,
    Shows his hot courage and his high desire.

Sometime he trots, as if he told the steps,
With gentle majesty and modest pride;
Anon he rears upright, curvets and leaps,
As who should say, 'Lo! thus my strength is tried;
    And this I do to captivate the eye
    Of the fair breeder that is standing by.'

What recketh he his rider's angry stir,
His flattering 'Holla', or his 'Stand, I say'?
What cares he now for curb or pricking spur,
For rich caparisons, or trapping gay?
    He sees his love, and nothing else he sees,
    Nor nothing else with his proud sight agrees.

Look, when a painter would surpass the life,
In limning out a well-proportion'd steed,
His art with nature's workmanship at strife,
As if the dead the living should exceed;
    So did this horse excel a common one,
    In shape, in courage, colour, pace, and bone.

Round-hoof'd, short-jointed, fetlocks shag and long,
Broad breast, full eye, small head, and nostril wide,
High crest, short ears, straight legs, and passing strong,
Thin mane, thick tail, broad buttock, tender hide:
 Look, what a horse should have he did not lack,
 Save a proud rider on so proud a back.

Sometime he scuds far off, and there he stares;
Anon he starts at stirring of a feather;
To bid the wind a base he now prepares,
And whether he run or fly they know not whether;
 For thro' his mane and tail the high wind sings,
 Fanning the hairs, who wave like feather'd wings."

In *Richard II.* (v. 5. 72) the dialogue between the
Groom and the King could have been written only by
one who knew by experience the affection that one
comes to feel for a favorite horse:—

" *Groom.* I was a poor groom of thy stable, king,
When thou wert king; who, travelling towards York,
With much ado at length have gotten leave
To look upon my sometimes royal master's face.
O, how it yearn'd my heart, when I beheld,
In London streets, that coronation day,
When Bolingbroke rode on roan Barbary,
That horse that thou so often hast bestrid,
That horse that I so carefully have dress'd !
 King Richard. Rode he on Barbary? Tell me, gentle
  friend,
How went he under him?
 Groom. So proud as if he had disdain'd the ground.
 King Richard. So proud that Bolingbroke was on his
  back !
That jade hath eat bread from my royal hand;
This hand hath made him proud with clapping him.

Would he not stumble? Would he not fall down,—
Since pride must have a fall,—and break the neck
Of that proud man that did usurp his back?
Forgiveness, horse! why do I rail on thee,
Since thou, created to be awed by man,
Wast born to bear? I was not made a horse;
And yet I bear a burden like an ass,
Spur-gall'd and tir'd by jauncing Bolingbroke."

The description of hare-hunting in *Venus and Adonis* (679) must also have been based on actual experience in the sport:—

" And when thou hast on foot the purblind hare,
Mark the poor wretch, to overshoot his troubles
How he outruns the winds, and with what care
He cranks and crosses with a thousand doubles:
    The many musits through the which he goes,
    Are like a labyrinth to amaze his foes.

" Sometime he runs among a flock of sheep,
To make the cunning hounds mistake their smell,
And sometime where earth-delving conies keep,
To stop the loud pursuers in their yell,
    And sometime sorteth with a herd of deer;
    Danger deviseth shifts, wit waits on fear:

" For there his smell with others being mingled,
The hot scent-snuffing hounds are driven to doubt,
Ceasing their clamorous cry till they have singled
With much ado the cold fault cleanly out;
    Then do they spend their mouths: Echo replies,
    As if another chase were in the skies.

" By this, poor Wat, far off upon a hill,
Stands on his hinder legs with listening ear,

To hearken if his foes pursue him still:
Anon their loud alarums he doth hear;
　And now his grief may be compared well
　To one sore sick that hears the passing-bell.

" Then shalt thou see the dew-bedabbled wretch
Turn, and return, indenting with the way;
Each envious brier his weary legs doth scratch,
Each shadow makes him stop, each murmur stay:
　For misery is trodden on by many
　And being low never reliev'd by any."

Mr. John R. Wise comments on this passage as follows: "This description of the run is wonderfully
true; how the 'dew-bedabbled wretch' betakes herself
to a flock of sheep to lead the hounds off the scent;
how she stops to listen, and again makes another
double. Mark, too, the beauty and aptness of the
epithets, 'the hot scent-snuffing' hounds, and the
'earth-delving' conies; but more especially mark the
pity that the poet feels for the poor animal, showing
that he possessed a true feeling heart, without which
no line of poetry can ever be written."

FOWLING.

There are many allusions to fowling in Shakespeare's
works. He had evidently seen a good deal of it, probably in his boyhood, whether he had had actual experience in it or not.

In *As You Like It* (v. 4. 111) the Duke says of
Touchstone, who combined much philosophy with his
professional foolery, " He uses his folly like a stalking-
horse, and under the presentation of that he shoots his

wit." And in *Much Ado About Nothing* (ii. 3. 95),
when Don Pedro and his companions are talking about
Benedick, whom they know to be hid within hearing,
Claudio says: "Stalk on, stalk on; the fowl sits";
that is, go on with the practical joke, for the victim
does not suspect it.

The stalking-horse, originally, was a horse trained
for the purpose and covered with trappings, so as to
conceal the sportsman from the game. It was particularly useful to the archer by enabling him to approach
the birds, without being seen by them, near enough to
reach them with his arrows. As it was not always
convenient to use a real horse for this purpose, the
fowler had recourse to an artificial one, made of stuffed
canvas and painted like a horse, but light enough to
be moved with one hand. Hence *stalking-horse* came
to be used figuratively for anything put forward to conceal a more important object, or to mask one's real in-
tention. Thus an old writer describes a hypocrite as
one "that makes religion his stalking-horse."

In the *Midsummer-Night's Dream* (iii. 2. 20) Puck, describing the fright of the clowns when Bottom makes his
appearance with the ass's head on his shoulders, says :—

> "Anon his Thisbe must be answered,
>   And forth my mimic comes. When they him spy,
>   As wild geese that the creeping fowler eye,
>   Or russet-pated choughs, many in sort,
>   Rising and cawing at the gun's report,
>   Sever themselves and madly sweep the sky,
>   So at his sight away his fellows fly."

In 1 *Henry IV.* (iv. 2. 21) Falstaff says that his recruits are "such as fear the report of a caliver [mus-

ket] worse than a struck fowl or a hurt wild-duck."
And in *Much Ado* (ii. 1. 209) Benedick says of Claudio,
who runs away from his friend's bantering: "Alas,
poor hurt fowl! now will he creep into sedges"; that
is, he will go and brood over his vexation in solitude.

In *The Tempest* (ii. 1. 85) we have an allusion to
"bat-fowling," a method of fowling by night in which
the birds were started from their nests and stupefied
by a sudden blaze of light from torches. Gervase
Markham, a contemporary of Shakespeare, in his *Hun-
ger's Prevention, or the Whole Arte of Fowling*, says: "I
think meet to proceed to Bat-fowling, which is likewise
a nighty taking of all sorts of great and small birds,
which rest not on the earth, but on shrubs, tall bushes,
hawthorn trees, and other trees, and may fitly and most
conveniently be used in all woody, rough, and bushy
countries, but not in the champaign," or open country.
He then goes on to explain how it is carried on. Some
of the sportsmen have torches to start the birds, while
others are armed with "long poles, very rough and
bushy at the upper ends," with which they beat down
the birds bewildered by the light and capture them.

HAWKING.

Hawking, or falconry, the art of training and flying
hawks for the purpose of catching other birds, was a
sport generally limited to the nobility; but Shakespeare's many allusions to it show that he was very
familiar with all its forms and its technicalities. He
doubtless saw a good deal of it in his boyhood rambles
in the neighborhood of Stratford.

The practice of hawking declined with the improve-

ment in muskets, which afforded a readier and surer
method of procuring game, with an equal degree of
out-of-door exercise. As the expense of training and
keeping hawks was very great, it is no wonder that the
gun soon superseded the bird with sportsmen. The
change, indeed, was surprisingly rapid. Hentzner, in
his *Itinerary*, written in 1598, tells us that hawking was
then the general sport of the English nobility; and
most of the best treatises upon this subject were written about that time; but in the latter part of the next
century the art was almost unknown.

Shakespeare knew all the different kinds of hawks.
He refers several times to the *haggard*, or wild hawk.
In *Much Ado* (iii. 1. 36) Hero says of Beatrice :—

> " I know her spirits are as coy and wild
> As haggards of the rock."

In *The Taming of the Shrew* (iv. 1. 196) Petruchio
employs the same figure with reference to Katharina :—

> " Another way I have to man my haggard,
> To make her come and know her keeper's call ";

where *man* means to tame. Again in the same play
(iv. 2. 39) the shrew is called "this proud disdainful
haggard."

The nestling or unfledged hawk was called an *eyas;*
and in *Hamlet* (ii. 2. 355) the boy actors, who were becoming popular when the play was written, are sneer-
ingly described as " an aery of children, little eyases."
In the *Merry Wives of Windsor* (iii. 3. 22), Mrs. Ford
addresses Robin, the page of Falstaff thus : " How now,

my eyas-musket! what news with you?" The eyas-
musket was the young sparrow-hawk, a small and in-

ELIZABETH HAWKING

ferior species of hawk. The word is derived from the
Latin *musca*, a fly, and probably refers to the small
size of the bird. It is curious that, as applied to the

firearm, it has the same origin. The gun was figuratively compared to the hawk as a means of taking
birds. Similarly, a kind of cannon used in the 16th
century was called a falcon; and another, of smaller
bore, was known as a *falconet*.

In *Romeo and Juliet* (ii. 2. 160), when the lover has
left his lady and she would call him back, she says :—

> " Hist, Romeo, hist! O for a falconer's voice
> To lure this tassel-gentle back again !"

The *tassel-gentle*, or *tercel-gentle*, was the male hawk.
Cotgrave, in his *French Dictionary* (edition of 1672)
defines *tiercelet* as " the Tassell or male of any kind of
Hawk, so termed because he is, commonly, a third part
less than the female." The *gentle* referred to the ease
with which the bird was trained.

We find the word *tercel* in *Troilus and Cressida* (iii.
2. 56): " The falcon as the tercel, for all the ducks in
the river "; that is, the female bird is as good as
the male.

The male bird, however, was seldom used in hawking, on account of its inferiority in size and strength.
In descriptions of the sport we find the female pronoun generally applied to the bird. Tennyson in
Lancelot and Elaine originally wrote :—

> " No surer than our falcon yesterday,
> Who lost the hern we slipt him at";

but he afterwards changed " him " to " her."

The hawk was " hooded," that is, had a hood put
over its head, until it was *slipped*, or let fly at the
game; and to this we have several allusions in Shakespeare.

In *Henry V.* (iii. 7. 121) the Constable, sneering at the Dauphin, says of his boasted valor : " Never any-body saw it but his lackey : 't is a hooded valour ; and when it appears it will bate." To *bate*, or *bait*, was to flutter the wings, as the bird did when unhooded. In this passage there is a pun on *bate* in this sense and as meaning to abate or diminish.

In *Othello* (iii. 3. 260), when the Moor has been told by Iago that Desdemona may be false, he says :—

> " If I do prove her haggard,
> " Though that her jesses were my dear heart-strings,
> I'd whistle her off and let her down the wind,
> To prey at fortune."

Here we have several hawking terms in a single sentence. *Haggard*, already mentioned, is used as an adjective, meaning wild or lawless. The *jesses* were straps of leather or silk attached to the foot of the hawk, by which the falconer held her. The bird was *whistled off* when first set free for flight ; and she was always let fly against the wind. If she flew with the wind behind her, she seldom returned. If therefore a hawk was for any reason to be dismissed, she was *let down the wind*, and from that time shifted for herself and *preyed at fortune*, or at random.

The legs of the hawk were adorned with two small bells, not both of the same sound but differing by a semitone. They were intended to frighten the game, so that it could be more readily caught. This is alluded to in *Lucrece*, 511 :—

> " Harmless Lucretia, marking what he tells
> With trembling fear, as fowl hear falcon's bells."

Touchstone also refers to the bells in *As You Like It* (iii. 3. 81): "As the ox hath his bow, sir, the horse his curb, and the falcon her bells, so man hath his desires." There is another figurative allusion to them in 3 *Henry VI.* i. 1. 47, where Warwick, boasting of his power, says:—

"Neither the king, nor he that loves him best,
The proudest he that holds up Lancaster,
Dares stir a wing if Warwick shake his bells."

In England *mews* is the name commonly given to a livery stable, or place where carriage horses are kept. The word has a curious connection with hawking. A bird was said to *mew*, when it moulted or changed its feathers. When hawks were moulting they were shut up in a cage or coop, which was called a *mew*. The royal stables in London got the name of *mews* because they were built where the mews of the king's hawks had been situated. This was done in the year 1537, the hawks being removed to another place. The word *mews*, being thus used for the royal stables, gradually came to be applied to other buildings of the kind.

It would take too much space to quote and explain all the allusions to hawking in Shakespeare's works. The few here given may serve as samples of this very interesting class of technical terms, most of which became obsolete when the art ceased to be practised.

Before dropping the subject, however, I may remind the young reader that many of the quotations here given to illustrate archery, hawking, and other ancient arts, sports, and games, also illustrate the fact that the figurative language of a period is affected by its manners and customs. The one needs to be known in

BOY WITH HAWK AND HOUNDS

order to understand the other. To take a fresh example, John Skelton, who lived in the time of Henry
VIII., refers to a lady thus :—

> "Merry Margaret,
>   As midsummer flower;
> Gentle as falcon,
>   Or hawk of the tower."

If we should compare a young lady nowadays to a falcon or a hawk, she would hardly take it as a compliment; and this very simile has been criticised by a writer who evidently did not understand it. He says: "We would rather be excused from wedding a lady of that ravenous class. This simile, we fear, was predictive of sharp nails after marriage." He forgets, or does not know, that this was written when, as we have learned, the art of hawking was in vogue. The trained falcons were as gentle and docile as any dove. They were domestic pets, and high-born ladies especially took delight in them. Shakespeare in his 91st Sonnet says :—

"Some glory in their birth, some in their skill,
 Some in their wealth, some in their bodies' force,
 Some in their garments, though new-fangled ill,
 Some in their hawks and hounds, some in their horse.
 *   *   *   *   *   *   *
 Thy love is better than high birth to me,
 Richer than wealth, prouder than garments' cost,
 Of more delight than hawks or horses be,
 And, having thee, of all men's pride I boast."

And in *Much Ado* (iii. 4. 54) when Beatrice sighs, Margaret asks: "For a hawk, a horse, or a husband?"

Commentators on Shakespeare, like the critic quoted above, have sometimes erred in their interpretation of a passage because they did not understand the fact or usage upon which a figure or allusion was founded.

THEATRICAL ENTERTAINMENTS.

When the players came to town I suspect that no Stratford boy was more delighted than William. John

Shakespeare, like his fellows in the town council, seems to have been a lover of the drama. When he was bailiff in 1569 he granted licenses for performances of the Queen's and the Earl of Worcester's companies.

The Queen's company received nine shillings and the Earl's twelvepence for their first entertainments, to which the public were admitted free. They doubtless gave others afterwards for which an entrance fee was charged.

Did John Shakespeare take the five-year-old William to see them act? He may have done so, for we know that in the city of Gloucester (only thirty miles from Stratford) a man took his little boy, born in the same year with Shakespeare, to a free dramatic performance similarly provided by the corporation. In his auto-biography, written in his old age, the person tells how he went to the show with his father and stood between his legs as he sat upon one of the benches.

The play was one of the "moralities" then in vogue, and the good man's quaint description of it is worth quoting as giving an idea of those curious dramas :—

"It was called The Cradle of Security, wherein was personated a king or some great prince, with his court-iers of several kinds, amongst which three ladies were in special grace with him ; and they, keeping him in delights and pleasures, drew him from his graver coun-sellors, . . . that, in the end, they got him to lie down in a cradle upon the stage, where these three ladies, joining in a sweet song, rocked him asleep that he snorted again ; and in the mean time closely [that is, secretly] conveyed under the clothes wherewithal he was covered a vizard, like a swine's snout, upon his

11

face, with three wire chains fastened thereunto, the other end whereof being holden severally by those three ladies, who fall to singing again, and then discovered [uncovered] his face that the spectators might see how they had transformed him, going on with their singing.

"Whilst all this was acting, there came forth of another door at the farthest end of the stage two old men, the one in blue with a sergeant-at-arms his mace on his shoulder, the other in red with a drawn sword in his hand and leaning with the other hand upon the other's shoulder; and so they two went along in a soft pace round about by the skirt of the stage, till at last they came to the cradle, when all the court was in the greatest jollity; and then the foremost old man with his mace struck a fearful blow upon the cradle, whereat all the courtiers, with the three ladies and the vizard, all vanished; and the desolate prince starting up barefaced, and finding himself thus sent for to judgment, made a lamentable complaint of his miserable case, and so was carried away by wicked spirits.

"This prince did personate in the moral the Wicked of the World; the three ladies, Pride, Covetousness, and Luxury [Lust]; the two old men, the End of the World and the Last Judgment.

"This sight took such impression in me that, when I came towards man's estate, it was as fresh in my memory as if I had seen it newly acted."

So far as the Stratford records show, the theatrical company of 1569 was the first that had visited the town, but afterwards players came thither almost every year.

How much they had to do in awakening a passion

for the drama in the breast of young William and shaping his subsequent career, we cannot guess; but "the boy is father of the man," and in all that we know of Shakespeare as a boy we can detect the germinal influences of many characteristics of the man, the poet, and the dramatist.

WILLIAM KEMP DANCING THE MORRIS

HIDE-AND-SEEK

THE BOUNDARY ELM

SAINT GEORGE'S DAY.

WE do not know the precise date of William Shakespeare's birth. That of his baptism is recorded in the
parish register at Stratford as the 26th of April, 1564.
It was a common practice then to baptize infants when
they were three days old, and it has therefore been
assumed that William was born on the 23d of April;
but the rule, if rule it can be called, was often varied
from, and we have not a particle of evidence that it
was followed in this instance. It should, moreover, be

understood that the 23d of April, as dates were then reckoned in England, corresponded to our 3d of May.

It would be pleasant to think that the poet made his first appearance on the stage of human life on that particular day, for it was Saint George's day, a great holiday and time of feasting throughout the kingdom, Saint George being the patron saint of England.

There is a book with which Shakespeare was doubtless familiar when he grew up—a collection of ancient stories made by Richard Johnson — in which Saint George figures as one of the " Seven Champions of Christendom."

From this book, as Mr. A. H. Wall tells us, we learn "how Saint George was imprisoned by the black King of Morocco, after he had fought so miraculously against the Saracens, and slain a frightful dragon, which had destroyed entire cities by the poison of its breath, and had every day devoured a beautiful virgin. Escaping from prison, he carried off a princess he had rescued from the monster, whom neither sword nor spear could pierce, and brought her to England, where the twain 'lived happily ever after,' in Warwickshire, where, sometime in the third century they died. The war-cry of England was 'Saint George !' as that of France was ' Montjoye Saint Denis !' ; and to this day ' by George !' is an exclamation derived from the ancient custom of swearing by that Saint.

" The ancient ballad of Saint George and the Dragon (printed in the Percy *Reliques*) tells us that the shire in which he died was that in which he first saw the light; that his mother expired while giving him birth ; that a weird lady of the woods stole him when an infant and educated him by magic power to become a great warrior ; and that on his person, prophetic of his future career and greatness, were three very mysterious marks—on one shoulder a cross, on the breast a dragon, and round one leg a garter. Their meanings were revealed when he fought so astoundingly as a crusader in the Holy Land, when he killed the magic dragon in Egypt, and rescued the King's daughter, Silene or Sabra, and, after his death, when Edward III. founded the knightly Order of the Garter, and made Saint George its patron.

"Centuries before that, the soldiers had adopted him as their special patron, as had also not a few of the old trade guilds. In some of the provincial towns and cities regulations for the annual ceremony of 'Riding the George' were enforced by penalties more or less severe. An ancestor of Shakespeare's, John Arden, of Warwickshire, 'bequethed his white harneis complete to the church of Ashton for a George to were it.' This was in the reign of the seventh Harry. . . . There was also an ancient play called 'The Holy Martyr St. George,' which, sadly degenerated in modern times, used to be played by rustics as a piece of coarse buffoonery."

The "Riding of Saint George" was forbidden by Henry VIII., but the custom was nevertheless kept up in out-of-the-way places even after Edward VI. had made more stringent laws against it.

It appears from the ancient records of the Guild that Stratford was one of the very last places in which the celebration was finally suppressed. Shakespeare in his boyhood doubtless saw it carried out with all its antique splendor. Mr. Wall gives the following description of the festival :—

"How great would be the preparations ! Old arms

and armor from the Guild's collection would be burnished up to be used by the town watch and the archers.   All sorts of choice dishes and rare wines would be in demand for mighty feasting.   The suit of white armor, of an antique pattern, which hung above the altar of Saint George, would be taken down and cleaned with reverential care, and from all the surrounding towns and villages, castles and mansions, guests would come flocking in, day after day, filling the numerous inns to overflowing.

"On *the* day, gravel would be spread along the procession's route, and barricades erected; house fronts would be adorned with plants and tapestry.   Chambers (small cannon) would be fired at daybreak, and great shouts of 'Saint George!' would drown the echoes of their explosions.   The Master of the Guild, its schoolmaster (a truly learned man), with the monitors and scholars of the Grammar School in their long blue gowns and flat caps, with the priests of the Guild Chapel, would all walk in the procession, with their Guild brothers and sisters, with representatives of the trades practised in the town, and even with the old Almshouse people, smiling and chattering and wagging their ancient heads.   Nobody would be forgotten who had a fair claim to be conspicuously remembered then. The 'Bedals' would be there of course in all their native dignity, solemn and severe.   The town 'waits' would 'discourse most excellent music' with drums and fifes and other cheek-distending wind-instruments. The bells in the church and chapel tower would be ringing out right jovial peals.   Then would come the town trumpeters marching before the High Bailiff, Aldermen, and Chamberlains, with their long furred scarlet robes, their chains of office, and the newly-gilded maces borne before them.

"Then, riding on horseback, his armor and drawn sword flashing back the rays of a fitful sun, would be seen the living representative of Saint George, with his great white plume floating from his white helm, as the soft, sweet, playing wind tossed it to and fro. Behind him, creating as he came such a roar of honest irre-pressible laughter as would have done your heart good to hear, would waddle the dragon (oh! such a dragon!) a 'property' one, with two boys inside it, led in chains, with the spear of Saint George down its throat. And then the vicar, his curates, and the gentry, in all the grandeur of silk and satin lace and spangles, would do the 'Riding' honor, with gold and silver chains about their necks, spurs at their heels, and swords by their sides, the Lord and Lady of the Manor riding before them. And these last-named were indeed dignitaries of great consequence, being, you must know, no lesser personages than Ambrose Dudley, 'the Good Earl' and his good lady, patrons of learning and rewarders of virtue, from their great castle at Warwick.

"But there is one feature of the Riding which must not on any account be forgotten. This was the Egyp-tian Princess, personated by the prettiest girl in Strat-ford (where pretty girls were always found, and are still not few). She came on a raised wheeled platform with a golden crown upon her head (made of gilded paste-board), and by her side a pretty pet lamb, garlanded with the earliest flowers of the spring, blushing (she, not the lamb) and smiling, and looking down very charming—as I tenderly imagine.

"And all the time they were passing, the bells would

ring out right merrily, and the people shout most lustily; and from every throat, blending thunderously, would come the cry, the cry that England's foes had trembled at in many a desperate fight: ' Saint George for England, Saint George for Merry England!'

"It was customary to announce this Riding by sound of trumpet from the Market Cross some time before it took place. And so I can fancy John Shakespeare, the glover, with all his clever work-people, men and women, artists and mechanics, joining the crowd that listens to the town trumpeter's loud-ringing voice here at the Cross, and opposite the Cage, where once lived Judith Shakespeare. By John, stands—in my fancy— Mary, his wife, with little Willie holding tightly to her hand, in a state of intense excitement; and almost before the crier has spoken his lines this laughing little fellow, who has been looking on with such wide-open wondering brown eyes, is suddenly lifted into the air and from above his father's head cries, in his child-ishly treble voice, 'Saint George for England!' for his mother had said, ' 'T is his right to lead the shouting here to-day, dear neighbors all, for on Saint George's day my boy was born.' "

EASTER.

The festival of Easter would generally come before Saint George's day. When Shakespeare was a boy the Reformation had somewhat mitigated the ancient rigor and austerity of Lent, but Easter was none the less a joyous and jubilant anniversary.

"Surely," as Mr. Charles Knight remarks, "there was something exquisitely beautiful in the old custom

of going forth into the fields before the sun had risen
on Easter-day, to see him mounting over the hills with
a tremulous motion, as if it were an animate thing
bounding in sympathy with the redeemed of mankind.
The young poet [Shakespeare] might have joined his
simple neighbors on this cheerful morning, and yet
have thought with Sir Thomas Browne, 'We shall not,
I hope, disparage the Resurrection of our Redeemer if
we say that the sun doth *not* dance on Easter-day.'
But one of the most glorious images of one of his early
plays [*Romeo and Juliet*] has given life and movement
to the sun :—

> "'Night's candles are burnt out, and *jocund* Day
> Stands *tiptoe* on the misty mountain's tops.'

Saw he not the sun dance—heard he not the expression of the undoubting belief that the sun danced—as
he went forth into Stratford meadows in the early twi-
light of Easter-day?"

Sir John Suckling, in his *Ballad upon a Wedding*,
alludes prettily to this old superstition in the description of the bride :—

> "But O she dances such a way !
> No sun upon an Easter day
> Is half so fine a sight."

Perhaps Shakespeare had this bit of folk-lore in
mind when he wrote these lines in *Coriolanus* (v.
4. 52) :—

> "The trumpets, sackbuts, psalteries and fifes,
> Tabors and cymbals and the shouting Romans,
> Make the sun dance."

Easter was a favorite time for games of ball and many of the athletic sports described in the preceding pages.

THE PERAMBULATION OF THE PARISH.

On the road to Henley-in-Arden, a few hundred yards from John Shakespeare's house in Henley Street, there stood until about fifty years ago an ancient boundary-tree—an elm to which reference is made in records of the 16th century. From that point the boundary of the borough continued to "the two elms in Evesham highway"; and so on, from point to point, round to the tree first mentioned. Once a year, in Rogation Week (six weeks after Easter), the clergy, the magistrates and public officers, and the inhabitants, including the boys of the Grammar School, assembled under this elm for the perambulation of the boundaries. They marched in procession, with waving banners and poles crowned with garlands, over the entire circuit of the parish limits. Under each "gospel-tree," as at the first boundary elm, a passage from Scripture was read, a collect recited, and a psalm sung.

These parochial processions were kept up after the Reformation. In 1575 a form of devotion for the "Rogation Days of Procession" was prescribed, "without addition of any superstitious ceremonies heretofore used"; and it was subsequently ordered that the curate on such occasions "shall admonish the people to give thanks to God in the beholding of God's benefits," and enforce the scriptural denunciations against those who remove their neighbors' landmarks. Izaak Walton tells how the pious Hooker encouraged these annual ceremonies: "He would by no means omit the customary time of procession, persuading all, both rich and poor, if they desired the preservation of love and their parish rights and liberties, to accompany him in his perambulation; and most did so: in which perambulation he would usually express more pleasant discourse than at other times, and would then always drop some loving and facetious observations, to be remembered against the next year, especially by the boys and young people; still inclining them, and all his present parishioners, to meekness and mutual kindnesses and love, because love thinks not evil, but covers a multitude of infirmities."

"And so," remarks Mr. Knight, after quoting this passage, "listening to the gentle words of some venerable Hooker of his time, would the young Shakespeare walk the bounds of his native parish. One day would not suffice to visit its numerous gospel-trees. Hours would be spent in reconciling differences among the cultivators of the common fields; in largesses to the poor; in merry-making at convenient halting-places. A wide parish is this of Stratford, including eleven villages and hamlets. A district of beautiful and varied scenery is this parish—hill and valley, wood and water. . . . For nearly three miles from Welcombe Greenhill the boundary lies along a wooded ridge, opening prospects of surpassing beauty. There may the distant spires of Coventry be seen peeping above the intermediate hills, and the nearer towers of Warwick lying cradled in their surrounding woods. . . . At the northern extremity of the high land, which principally belongs to the estate of Clopton, and which was doubtless a park in early times, we have a panoramic

view of the valley in which Stratford lies, with its
hamlets of Bishopton, Little Wilmecote, Shottery, and
Drayton. As the marvellous boy of the Stratford
Grammar School then looked upon that plain, how
little could he have foreseen the course of his future
life ! For twenty years of his manhood he was to have
no constant dwelling-place in that his native town ; but
it was to be the home of his affections. He would be
gathering fame and opulence in an almost untrodden
path, of which his young ambition could shape no definite image ; but in the prime of his life he was to
bring his wealth to his own Stratford, and become the
proprietor and the contented cultivator of the loved
fields that he now saw mapped out at his feet. Then,
a little while, and an early tomb under that grey tower
—a tomb so to be honored in all ages to come

"'That kings for such a tomb would wish to die.'"

MAY-DAY AND THE MORRIS-DANCE.

The first of May was in the olden time one of
the most delightful of holidays ; but its harmless
sports were an abomination in the eyes of the Puritans. Philip Stubbes, in his *Anatomie of Abuses* (1583)
says : " Against May, every parish, town, and village
assemble themselves together, both men, women, and
children, old and young, even all indifferently : and
either going all together, or dividing themselves into
companies, they go, some to the woods and groves,
some to the hills and mountains, some to one place,
some to another, where they spend all the night in
pastimes ; and in the morning they return, bringing
with them birch boughs and branches of trees to deck

their assemblies withal. . . . But their chiefest jewel they bring from thence is their *May pole*, which they bring home with great veneration, as thus:—They have twenty or forty yoke of oxen, every ox having a sweet nosegay of flowers tied on the tip of his horns, and these oxen draw home this May pole, which is covered all over with flowers and herbs, bound round about with strings, from the top to the bottom, and sometime painted with variable colors, with two or three hundred men, women, and children following it, with great devotion. And thus being reared up, with handkerchiefs and flags streaming on the top, they strew the ground about, bind green boughs about it, set up summer halls, bowers, and arbors hard by it. And then fall they to banquet and feast, to leap and dance about it, as the heathen people did at the dedication of their idols, whereof this is a perfect pattern, or rather the thing itself."

Milton, though a Puritan, writes in a different vein in his *Song on May Morning:*—

" Now the bright morning-star, day's harbinger,
　　Comes dancing from the East, and leads with her
　　The flowery May, who from her green lap throws
　　The yellow cowslip and the pale primrose.
　　Hail, bounteous May, that dost inspire
　　Mirth and youth and warm desire!
　　Woods and groves are of thy dressing,
　　Hill and dale doth boast thy blessing.
　　Thus we salute thee with our early song,
　　And welcome thee, and wish thee long."

Kings and queens did not disdain to join in these rural sports. Henry VIII. and Queen Katherine en-

joyed them ; and he, in the early part of his reign, rose
on May Day very early and went with his courtiers to
the wood to "fetch May," or green boughs. In the
Midsummer-Night's Dream (iv. 1.) Theseus, Hippolyta,
and their train are in the wood in "the vaward of the
day," and find the pairs of lovers sleeping under the
influence of Puck's magic ; and Theseus says :—

> " No doubt they rose up early to observe
> The rite of May, and, hearing our intent,
> Came here in grace of our solemnity."

The boys and girls, as the sour Stubbes has told us,
were not slack to observe this rite of May. In a manuscript in the British Museum, entitled *The State of
Eton School*, and dated 1560, we read that "on the day
of Saint Philip and Saint James [May 1st], if it be fair
weather, and the master grants leave, those boys who
choose it may rise at four o'clock, to gather May
branches, if they can do it without wetting their feet:
and that on that day they adorn the windows of the
bedchamber with green leaves, and the houses are per-
fumed with fragrant herbs."

The May-pole was often kept standing from year to
year on the village green or in some public place in
town or city, and in such cases was usually painted
with various colors. One described by Tollet was
"painted yellow and black in spiral lines." In the
Midsummer-Night's Dream (iii. 2. 296), Hermia sneers
at the taller Helena as a "painted May-pole."

In *Henry VIII.* (v. 4. 15) when the Porter is angry
at the crowds that have made their way into the palace
yard, and calls for "a dozen crab-tree staves" to drive
them out, a man says to him :—

" Pray, sir, be patient: 't is as much impossible—
  Unless we sweep 'em from the door with cannons—
  To scatter 'em, as 't is to make 'em sleep
  On May-day morning; which will never be."

Of course the day was a holiday in the Stratford
school, and we may be sure that William made the
most of it.

An important feature in the May-day games in
Shakespeare's time was the *Morris-Dance*, in which a
group of characters associated with the stories of Robin Hood were the chief actors. These were Robin
himself; his faithful companion, Little John; Friar
Tuck, to whom Drayton alludes as

" Tuck the merry friar which many a sermon made
  In praise of Robin Hood, his outlaws and their trade;"

Maid Marian, the mistress of Robin; the Fool, who
was like the domestic buffoon of the time, with motley
dress, the cap and bells, and additional bells tied to his
arms and ankles; the Piper, sometimes called Tom Piper, the musician of the troop; and the Hobby-horse,
represented by a man equipped with a pasteboard frame
forming the head and hinder parts of a horse, with a
long mantle or footcloth reaching nearly to the ground,
to hide the man's legs; and the Dragon, another paste-
board device, much like the one in the Riding of Saint
George described above (page 169). In addition to
these characters there were a number of common dancers, in fantastic costume, with bells about their feet.

The forms and number of the characters varied
much with time and place. Sometimes only one or

two of those just mentioned were introduced in the dance, and sometimes others were added.

During the reign of Elizabeth the Puritans, by their sermons and invectives, did much to interfere with this feature of the May-day games. Friar Tuck was deemed a remnant of Popery, and the Hobby-horse an impious superstition. The opposition to them became so bitter that they were generally omitted from the sport. Allusions to the omission of the Hobby-horse are frequent in the plays of the time; as in *Love's Labour 's Lost* (iii. 1. 30): "The hobby-horse is forgot;" and *Hamlet* (iii. 2. 142): "or else he shall suffer not thinking on, with the hobby-horse, whose epitaph is, 'For, O, for, O, the hobby-horse is forgot.'" This "epitaph" (which is also referred to in *Love's Labour 's Lost*) appears to be a quotation from some popular song of the time. So in Beaumont and Fletcher's *Women Pleased* (iv. 1.) we find: "Shall the hobby-horse be forgot then?" and in Ben Jonson's *Entertainment at Althorp:* "But see, the hobby-horse is forgot."

Friar Tuck is alluded to by Shakespeare in *The Two Gentlemen of Verona* (iv. 1. 36), where one of the Outlaws who have seized Valentine exclaims :—

"By the bare scalp of Robin Hood's fat friar,
This fellow were a king for our wild faction!"

That he kept his place in the morris-dance in the reign of Elizabeth is evident from Warner's *Albion's England*, published in 1586: "Tho' Robin Hood, little John, friar Tuck, and Marian deftly play"; but he is not heard of afterwards. In Ben Jonson's *Masque of the Gipsies*, written about 1620, the Clown notes his absence from the dance: "There is no Maid Marian nor Friar amongst them."

Maid Marian also officiated as the Queen or Lady of the May, who had figured in the May-day festivities long before Robin Hood was introduced into them. She was probably at first the representative of the goddess Flora in the ancient Roman festival celebrated at the same season of the year.

Maid Marian was sometimes personated by a young woman, but oftener by a boy or young man in feminine dress. Later, when the morris-dance had degenerated into coarse foolery, the part was taken by a clown. In 1 *Henry IV.* (iii. 3. 129), Falstaff refers contemptuously to "Maid Marian" as a low character, which she had doubtless become by the time (1596 or 1597) when that play was written.

The connection of the morris-dance with May-day is alluded to in *All's Well that Ends Well* (ii. 2. 25): "as fit . . . as a morris for May-day"; but it came to be a feature of many other holidays and festivals, and was often one of the sports introduced to amuse the crowd at fairs and similar gatherings.

Mr. Knight gives us this fancy picture of the May-day games as they probably were in Shakespeare's boyhood :—

"An impatient group is gathered under the shade of the old elms, for the morning sun casts his slanting beams dazzlingly across the green. There is the distant sound of tabor and bagpipe:—

"'Hark, hark! I hear the dancing,
And a nimble morris prancing;

> The bagpipe and the morris bells
> That they are not far hence us tells.'

From out of the leafy Arden are they bringing in the
May-pole. The oxen move slowly with the ponderous
wain; they are garlanded, but not for the sacrifice.
Around the spoil of the forest are the pipers and the
dancers—maidens in blue kirtles, and foresters in green
tunics. Amidst the shouts of young and old, childhood
leaping and clapping its hands, is the May-pole raised.
But there are great personages forthcoming — not so
great, however, as in more ancient times. There are
Robin Hood and Little John, in their grass-green tunics;
but their bows and their sheaves of arrows are more for
show than use. Maid Marian is there; but she is a mock-
ery—a smooth-faced youth in a watchet-colored tunic,
with flowers and coronets, and a mincing gait, but not the
shepherdess who

> " ' with garlands gay
> Was made the Lady of the May.'

There is farce amidst the pastoral. The age of unreali-
ties has already in part arrived. Even among country-
folk there is burlesque. There is personation, with a
laugh at the things that are represented. The Hobby-
horse and the Dragon, however, produce their shouts of
merriment. But the hearty morris-dancers soon spread a
spirit of genial mirth among all the spectators. The
clownish Maid Marian will now 'caper upright like a wild
Morisco.' Friar Tuck sneaks away from his ancient companions to join hands with some undisguised maiden;
the Hobby-horse gets rid of pasteboard and his footcloth; and the Dragon quietly deposits his neck and tail
for another season. Something like the genial chorus of
Summer's Last Will and Testament is rung out:—

> " ' Trip and go, heave and ho,
> Up and down, to and fro,
> From the town to the grove,
> Two and two, let us rove,
> A-Maying, a-playing;
> Love hath no gainsaying,
> So merrily trip and go.'

"The early-rising moon still sees the villagers on that green of Shottery. The Piper leans against the May-pole; the featliest of dancers still swim to the music:—

> " ' So have I seen
> Tom Piper stand upon our village-green,
> Backed with the May-pole, whilst a jocund crew
> In gentle motion circularly threw
> Themselves around him.'

The same beautiful writer—one of the last of our golden age of poetry—has described the parting gifts bestowed upon the 'merry youngsters' by

> " ' the Lady of the May
> Set in an arbor (on a holiday)
> Built by the May-pole, where the jocund swains
> Dance with the maidens to the bagpipe's strains,
> When envious night commands them to be gone.' "

These latter quotations are from William Browne's *Britannia's Pastorals* (book ii. published in 1616), and the poet goes on to tell how the Lady

> "Calls for the merry youngsters one by one,
> And, for their well performance, soon disposes
> To this a garland interwove with roses;

To that a carved hook or well-wrought scrip;
Gracing another with her cherry lip;
To one her garter; to another then
A handkerchief cast o'er and o'er again:
And none returneth empty that hath spent
His pains to fill their rural merriment."

WHITSUNTIDE.

Whitsuntide, the season of Pentecost, or the week
following Whitsunday (the seventh Sunday after Easter), was another period of festivity in old English times.

The morris-dance was commonly one of its features,
as of the May-day sports. In *Henry V.* (ii. 4. 25) the
Dauphin alludes to it:—

" ' I say 't is meet we all go forth
To view the sick and feeble parts of France;
And let us do it with no show of fear,
No, with no more than if we heard that England
Were busied with a Whitsun morris-dance."

Another custom connected with the festival was the
" Whitsun-ale." Ale was so common a drink in England that it became a part of the name of various festal meetings. A " leet-ale " was a feast at the holding
of a court-leet; a " lamb-ale " was a sheep-shearing
merry-making; a " bride-ale" was a *bridal,* as we now
call it—always a festive occasion; and a "church-ale "
was connected with some ecclesiastical holiday.

John Aubrey, the eminent antiquary, writing in the
latter part of the 17th century, says that in his grandfather's days the church-ale at Whitsuntide furnished
all the money needed for the relief of the parish poor.

He adds: "In every parish is, or was, a church-house, to which belonged spits, crocks, etc., utensils for dressing provision. Here the housekeepers met and were merry, and gave their charity. The young people were there too, and had dancing, bowling, shooting at butts, without scandal."

The Puritan Stubbes, in the book before quoted (page 176, above), took a different view of these social gatherings. He says: "In certain towns, where drunken Bacchus bears sway, against Christmas and Easter, Whitsuntide, or some other time, the churchwardens of every parish, with the consent of the whole parish, provide half a score or twenty quarters of malt, whereof some they buy of the church stock, and some is given them of the parishioners themselves, every one conferring somewhat, according to his ability; which malt, being made into very strong ale or beer, is set to sale, either in the church or some other place assigned to that purpose. Then when this is set abroach, well is he that can get the soonest to it, and spend the most at it."

Old parish records show that considerable money was obtained at these festivals, not only by the sale of ale and food, but from the charges made for certain games, among which "riffeling" (raffling) is included. Neighboring parishes often united in these church picnics, as they might be called. Richard Carew, in his *Survey of Cornwall* (1602), says: "The neighboring parishes at these times lovingly visit one another, and this way frankly spend their money together."

Whitsuntide was also a favorite time for theatrical performances. Long before Shakespeare's day the miracle-plays and moralities had been popular at this season; and these, as we have seen (page 17), were still kept up when he was a boy, together with "pastorals" and other "pageants" such as Perdita alludes to in *The Winter's Tale* (iv. 4. 134):—

> "Come, take your flowers:
> Methinks I play as I have seen them do
> In Whitsun pastorals;"

and such as the disguised Julia describes in *The Two Gentlemen of Verona* (iv. 4. 163):—

> "At Pentecost,
> When all our pageants of delight were play'd,
> Our youth got me to play the woman's part,
> And I was trimm'd in Madam Julia's gown,
> Which served me as fit, by all men's judgments,
> As if the garment had been made for me;
> Therefore, I know she is about my height.
> And at that time I made her weep a-good,
> For I did play a lamentable part.
> Madam, 't was Ariadne, passioning
> For Theseus' perjury and unjust flight,
> Which I so lively acted with my tears
> That my poor mistress, moved therewithal,
> Wept bitterly; and would I might be dead
> If I in thought felt not her very sorrow!"

This is in one of the earliest of his plays, and may be a reminiscence of some simple attempt at dramatic representation which he had seen at Stratford.

MIDSUMMER EVE.

The Vigil of Saint John the Baptist, or the evening before the day (June 24) dedicated to that Saint, was commonly called Midsummer Eve, and was observed with curious ceremonies in all parts of England. On that evening the people used to go into the woods and break down branches of trees, which they brought home and fixed over their doors with great demonstrations of joy. This was originally done to make good the Scripture prophecy concerning the Baptist, that many should rejoice in his birth.

It was also customary on this occasion for old and young, of both sexes, to make merry about a large bonfire made in the street or some open place. They danced around it, and the young men and boys leaped over it, not to show their agility, but in compliance with an ancient custom. These diversions they kept up till midnight, and sometimes later.

According to some old writers these fires were made because the Saint was said in Holy Writ to be "a shining light." Others, while not denying this, added that the fires served to drive away the dragons and evil spirits hovering in the air; and one asserts that in some countries bones were burnt in this "bonefire," or bonfire, "for the dragons hated nothing more than the stench of burning bones."

In the *Ordinary of the Company of Cooks* at Newcastle-upon-Tyne, 1575, we read among other regulations: "And also that the said Fellowship of Cooks shall yearly of their own cost and charge maintain and keep the bone-fires, according to the ancient custom of the town on the Sand-hill; that is to say, one bone-fire on the Even of the Feast of the Nativity of St. John the Baptist, commonly called Midsummer Even, and the other on the Even of the Feast of St. Peter the Apostle, if it shall please the mayor and aldermen of the town for the time being to have the same bone-fires."

In a manuscript record of the expenses of the royal household for the first year of the reign of Henry VIII. (1513), under date of July 1st is the entry: "Item, to the pages of the hall, for making of the King's bone-fire upon Midsummer Eve, x*s*."

There were many popular superstitions connected with Midsummer Eve. It was believed that if any one sat up fasting all night in the church porch, he would see the spirits of those who were to die in the parish during the ensuing twelve months come and knock at the church door, in the order in which they were to die.

It was customary on this evening to gather certain plants which were supposed to have magical properties. Fern-seed, for instance, being on the back of the leaf and in some species hardly discernible, was thought to have the power of rendering the possessor invisible, if it was gathered at this time. In some places it was believed that the seed must be got at midnight by letting it fall into a plate without touching the plant.

We find many allusions to fern-seed in Elizabethan writers. In 1 *Henry IV.* (ii. 1. 95) Gadshill says: "We steal as in a castle, cock-sure; we have the receipt of fern-seed, we walk invisible"; to which the Chamberlain replies: "Nay, by my faith, I think ye are more beholding to the night than to fern-seed for your walking invisible." In Ben Jonson's *New Inn* (i. 1) one of the characters says:—

> "I had
> No medicine, sir, to go invisible,
> No fern-seed in my pocket."

In *Plaine Percevall*, a tract of the time of Elizabeth, we read: "I think the mad slave hath tasted on a fern-stalk, that he walks so invisible."

Scot, in his *Discoverie of Witchcraft* (1584), directs us, as protection against witches, to "hang boughs (hallowed on Midsummer Day) at the stall door where the cattle stand."

St. John's wort, vervain, orpine, and rue were among the plants gathered on Midsummer Eve on account of their supernatural virtue. Each was supposed to have its peculiar use in popular magic. Orpine, for instance, was set in clay upon pieces of slate, and called a "Midsummer man." According as the stalk was found next morning to incline to the right or the left, the anxious maiden knew whether her lover would prove true to her or not. Young women also sought at this time for what they called pieces of coal, but in reality hard, black, dead roots, often found under the living mugwort; and these they put under their pillows that they might dream of their lovers. Lupton, in his *Notable Things* (1586), says: "It is certainly and constantly affirmed that on Midsummer Eve there is found, under the root of mugwort, a coal which saves or keeps them safe from the plague, carbuncle, lightning, the quartan ague, and from burning, that bear the same about them." He also says it is reported that the same remarkable "coal" is found at the same time of the year under the root of plantain; and he adds that he knows this "to be of truth," for he has found it there himself!

Midsummer Eve was also thought to be a season productive of madness. In *Twelfth Night* (iii. 4. 61) Olivia says of Malvolio's eccentric behavior, "Why, this

is very midsummer madness." Steevens, the Shakespearian critic, believed that the *Midsummer-Night's
Dream* owed its title to this association of mental va-
garies with the season. John Heywood, writing in the
latter part of the 16th century, alludes to the same
belief when he says :—

"As mad as a March hare ; when madness compares,
 Are not Midsummer hares as mad as March hares ?"

It is not improbable, however, that the *Midsummer-
Night's Dream* was so called because it was to be first
represented at Midsummer, or because it was like the
plays commonly performed in connection with the festivities of that season. A drama in which fairies were
leading characters was in keeping with the time of
year when fairies and spirits were supposed to manifest themselves to mortal vision either in vigils or in
dreams.

CHRISTMAS.

Passing by sundry minor festivals of the year, we
come to Christmas, which is a day of feasting and
merrymaking in England even now, though but a
" starveling Christmas " compared with that of the
olden time. "Where now," as Mr. Knight asks, "is
the real festive exhilaration of Christmas ; the meeting
of all ranks as children of a common father ; the tenant
speaking freely in his landlord's hall ; the laborers and
their families sitting at the same great oak table ; the
Yule Log brought in with shout and song? 'No night
is now with hymn or carol blest.' There are singers
of carols even now at a Stratford Christmas. War-

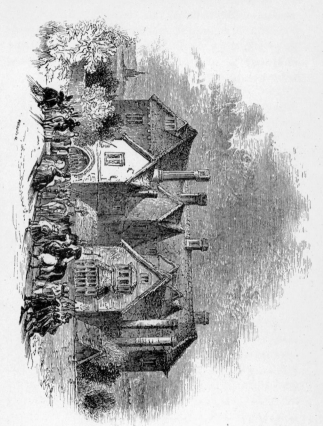

CLOPTON HOUSE ON CHRISTMAS EVE

wickshire has retained some of its ancient carols. But
the singers are wretched chorus-makers, according to
the most unmusical style of all the generations from
the time of the Commonwealth. . . . But in an age of
music we may believe that one young dweller in Stratford gladly woke out of his innocent sleep, after the
evening bells had rung him to rest, when in the still-
ness of the night the psaltery was gently touched before his father's porch, and he heard, one voice under
another, these simple and solemn strains :—

> " ' As Joseph was a-walking
> He heard an angel sing,
> This night shall be born
> Our heavenly King.

> " ' He neither shall be born
> In housen nor in hall,
> Nor in the place of Paradise,
> But in an ox's stall.

> " ' He neither shall be clothed
> In purple nor in pall,
> But all in fair linen,
> As were babies all.

> " ' He neither shall be rock'd
> In silver nor in gold,
> But in a wooden cradle
> That rocks on the mould.'

London has perhaps this carol yet, among its halfpenny ballads. A man who had a mind attuned to
the love of what was beautiful in the past has pre-

served it; but it was for another age. It was for the
age of William Shakespeare. It was for the age when
superstition, as we call it, had its poetical faith. . . .

"Such a night was a preparation for a 'happy Christmas.' The Cross of Stratford was garnished with the
holly, the ivy, and the bay. Hospitality was in every
house; but the hall of the great landlord of the parish
was a scene of rare conviviality. The frost or the
snow will not deter the principal tenants and friends
from the welcome of Clopton. There is the old house,
nestled in the woods, looking down upon the little
town. Its chimneys are reeking; there is bustle in the
offices; the sound of the trumpeters and the pipers is
heard through the open door of the great entrance;
the steward marshals the guests; the tables are fast
filling. Then advance, courteously, the master and
the mistress of the feast. The Boar's head is brought
in with due solemnity; the wine-cup goes round; and
perhaps the Saxon shout of Waes-hael and Drink-hael
may still be shouted. The boy-guest who came with
his father, the tenant of Ingon, has slid away from the
rout; for the steward, who loves the boy, has a sight
to make him merry. The Lord of Misrule and his
jovial attendants are rehearsing their speeches; and
the mummers from Stratford are at the porch. Very
sparing are the cues required for the enactment of this
short drama. A speech to the esquire, closed with a
merry jest; something about ancestry and good Sir
Hugh; the loud laugh; the song and the chorus; and
the Lord of Misrule is now master of the feast. The
Hall is cleared. . . . There is dancing till curfew; and
then a walk in the moonlight to Stratford, the pale
beam shining equally upon the dark resting place in

the lonely aisle of the Clopton who is gone, and upon the festal hall of the Clopton who remains, where some loiterers of the old and young still desire 'to burn this night with torches.' "

This is a fancy picture, but it is in keeping with the life of the time. Whether the boy Shakespeare spent a Christmas in just this manner or not, we may be sure that he enjoyed the merriment of the season to the full.

There are a few allusions to Christmas in the plays, besides the beautiful one in *Hamlet* already quoted (page 138) in another connection. In *Love's Labour 's Lost* (v. 2. 462) "a Christmas comedy" is alluded to; and in *The Taming of the Shrew* (ind. 2. 140), when Sly the tinker learns that a comedy is to be played for his entertainment, he asks whether a "comonty" is "like a Christmas gambold or a tumbling-trick."

SHEEP-SHEARING.

Our English ancestors had other holidays than those associated with the ecclesiastical year, but only one or two of them can be mentioned here.

The time of sheep-shearing was celebrated by a rural feast such as Shakespeare has introduced in *The Winter's Tale*. The shearing took place in the spring as soon as the weather became warm enough for the sheep to lay aside their winter clothing without danger. John Dyer, in his poem entitled *The Fleece* (1757), fixes the proper time thus:—

> " If verdant elder spreads
> Her silver flowers, if humble daisies yield
> To yellow crowfoot and luxuriant grass,
> Gay shearing-time approaches."

13

Drayton, writing in Shakespeare's day (page 3 above),
describes a shearing-feast in the Vale of Evesham, not
far from Stratford :—

> "The shepherd-king,
> Whose flock hath chanced that year the earliest lamb
>   to bring,
> In his gay baldric sits at his low, grassy board,
> With flawns, curds, clouted cream, and country dainties
>   stored ;
> And whilst the bagpipe plays, each lusty jocund swain
> Quaffs syllabubs in cans to all upon the plain ;
> And to their country girls, whose nosegays they do
>   wear,
> Some roundelays do sing, the rest the burden bear."

In *The Winter's Tale*, instead of the shepherd-king
we have the more poetical shepherdess-queen. Dr. F.
J. Furnivall, in his introduction to this play, remarks :
" How happily it brings Shakespeare before us, mixing
with his Stratford neighbors at their sheep-shearing
and country sports, enjoying the vagabond peddler's
gammon and talk, delighting in the sweet Warwickshire maidens, and buying them 'fairings,' opening his
heart afresh to all the innocent mirth and the beauty
of nature around him !" Doubtless he enjoyed these
rural festivities in his later years, after he settled down
in his own house at Stratford, no less heartily than he
did in his boyhood, when his father may have had
sheep to shear.

Mr. Knight remarks : " There is a minuteness of circumstance amidst the exquisite poetry of this scene [in
The Winter's Tale] which shows that it must have been
founded upon actual observation, and in all likelihood

upon the keen and prying observation of a boy occupied and interested with such details. Surely his father's pastures and his father's homestead might have supplied all these circumstances. His father's man might be the messenger to the town, and reckon upon 'counters' the cost of the sheep-shearing feast. 'Three pounds of sugar, five pounds of currants, rice'—and then he asks, 'What will this sister of mine do with rice?' In Bohemia the clown might, with dramatic propriety, not know the use of rice at a sheep-shearing; but a Warwickshire swain would have the flavor of cheese-cakes in his mouth at the first mention of rice and currants. Cheese-cakes and warden-pies were the sheep-shearing delicacies."

Shakespeare evidently knew for what the rice was wanted at the feast; but the clown, who was no cook, might be familiar with the flavor of the cakes without understanding all the ingredients that entered into their composition.

Thomas Tusser, in his *Five Hundred Points of Husbandry* (1557), describing this festival, makes the shepherd say :—

" Wife, make us a dinner, spare flesh neither corn,
Make wafers and cakes, for our sheep must be shorn ;
At sheep-shearing, neighbors none other things crave
But good cheer and welcome like neighbors to have."

HARVEST-HOME.

The ingathering of the harvest was a season of great rejoicing from the most remote antiquity. " Sowing is hope ; reaping, fruition of the expected good." To the husbandman to whom the fear of wet, blights, and other mischances has been a source of anxiety between seedtime and harvest, the fortunate completion of his long labors cannot fail to be a relief and a delight.

Paul Hentzner, writing in 1598 at Windsor, says: "As we were returning to our inn we happened to meet some country-people celebrating their harvest-home. Their last load of corn they crown with flowers, having besides an image richly dressed, by which perhaps they would signify Ceres. This they keep moving about, while men and women, riding through the streets in the cart, shout as loud as they can till they arrive at the barn." In the reign of James I., Moresin, another foreigner, saw a figure made of corn drawn home in a cart, with men and women singing to the pipe and the drum.

Matthew Stevenson, in the *Twelve Months* (1661), under August, alludes to this festival thus: "The furmenty-pot welcomes home the harvest-cart, and the garland of flowers crowns the captain of the reapers; the battle of the field is now stoutly fought. The pipe and the tabor are now busily set a-work; and the lad and the lass will have no lead on their heels. O, 't is the merry time wherein honest neighbors make good cheer, and God is glorified in his blessings on the earth."

Robert Herrick, in his *Hesperides* (1648), refers to the harvest-home as follows:—

"Come, sons of summer, by whose toil
  We are the lords of wine and oil,
  By whose tough labor and rough hands
  We rip up first, then reap our lands.

Crown'd with the ears of corn, now come,
And to the pipe sing harvest-home.
Come forth, my lord, and see the cart,
Drest up with all the country art.
See here a mawkin, there a sheet
As spotless pure as it is sweet:
The horses, mares, and frisking fillies
Clad all in linen, white as lilies;
The harvest swains and wenches bound
For joy to see the hock-cart crown'd.
About the cart hear how the rout
Of rural younglings raise the shout;
Pressing before, some coming after,
Those with a shout, and these with laughter.
Some bless the cart, some kiss the sheaves,
Some prank them up with oaken leaves;
Some cross the fill-horse; some, with great
Devotion, stroke the home-borne wheat.
*   *   *   *   *   *   *
Well, on, brave boys, to your lord's hearth,
Glittering with fire; where, for your mirth,
You shall see, first, the large and chief
Foundation of your feast, fat beef;
With upper stories, mutton, veal,
And bacon (which makes full the meal),
With several dishes standing by,
And here a custard, there a pie,
And here all-tempting frumenty."

The "hock-cart" was the cart that brought home the last load of corn. It was sometimes called the "hockey-cart"; and one of the dainties of the feast was the "hockey-cake." In an almanac for 1676, under August, we read:—

"Hocky is brought home with hallowing,
    Boys with plum-cake the cart following."

The harvest-home is alluded to in 1 *Henry IV.* (i. 3.
35), where Hotspur, describing the "popinjay" lord
who came to demand his prisoners, says :—

> "and his chin new-reap'd
> Show'd like a stubble-land at harvest-home."

In *The Merry Wives of Windsor* (ii. 2. 287) Falstaff
says of Mistress Ford, to whom he intends to make
love, "and there 's my harvest-home."

In the interlude in *The Tempest* (iv. 1. 134) the dance
of the Reapers was apparently a reminiscence of
harvest-home sports.   Iris says :—

> "You sunburnt sicklemen, of August weary,
>   Come hither from the furrow and be merry.
>   Make holiday; your rye-straw hats put on,
>   And these fresh nymphs encounter every one
>   In country footing."

The following passage in the 12th Sonnet, though it
has nothing of festival joyousness, may have been suggested by the ceremonial bringing home of the last
load of grain :—

> "When lofty trees I see barren of leaves
>   Which erst from heat did canopy the herd,
>   *And summer's green all girded up in sheaves*
>   *Borne on the bier with white and bristly beard,*" etc.

MARKETS AND FAIRS.

In a quiet country town like Stratford the weekly
market was an occasion of some interest to the boys as

to their elders. There is still such a market on Fridays at Stratford, when wares of many sorts are exposed for sale in the streets, and people from the neighboring villages come to buy. In old times there would have been a greater throng of buyers and sellers. "The housewife from her little farm would ride in gallantly between her paniers laden with butter, eggs, chickens, and capons. The farmer would stand by his pitched corn, and, as Harrison complains, if the poor man handled the sample with the intent to purchase his humble bushel, the man of many sacks would declare that it was sold. There, before shops were many and their stocks extensive, would come the dealers from Birmingham and Coventry, with wares for use and wares for show, — horse-gear and women-gear, Sheffield whittles, and rings with posies."

We find a number of allusions to these markets in Shakespeare's plays. In *Love's Labour's Lost* (v. 2. 318) Biron, ridiculing Boyet, says of him :—

"He is art's pedler, and retails his wares
    At wakes and wassails, meetings, markets, fairs."

In the same play (iii. 1. 111) there is an allusion to the old proverb, "Three women and a goose make a market," where Costard, referring to Moth's nonsense about "the fox, the ape, and the humble-bee," followed by the goose that made up four, says, "And he [the goose] ended the market."

In *As You Like It* (iii. 2. 104) Touchstone, making fun of Orlando's verses which Rosalind has just read, says: "I'll rhyme you so eight years together, dinners and suppers and sleeping-hours excepted : it is the right butter-women's rank to market"; that is, the metre is just like the jog-trot of countrywomen riding to market one after another, with their butter and eggs.

In *Richard III.* (i. 1. 160) Gloster, after saying that he means to "marry Warwick's youngest daughter," adds:—

"But yet I run before my horse to market:
Clarence still breathes, Edward still lives and reigns;
When they are gone, then must I count my gains."

He means, in the language of a more familiar proverb, that he is counting his chickens before they are hatched; that is, he is too hasty in reckoning upon the success of his plans.

In 1 *Henry VI.* (iii. 2) Joan of Arc gets into Rouen with her soldiers in the guise of countrymen bound for market:—

"*Enter* La Pucelle, *disguised, and* Soldiers *dressed like countrymen, with sacks upon their backs.*

Pucelle. These are the city gates, the gates of Rouen,
Through which our policy must make a breach.
Take heed, be wary how you place your words;
Talk like the vulgar sort of market-men,
That come to gather money for their corn.
If we have entrance—as I hope we shall—
And that we find the slothful watch but weak,
I'll by a sign give notice to our friends
That Charles the Dauphin may encounter them.

1 *Soldier.* Our sacks shall be a mean to sack the city,
And we be lords and rulers over Rouen;
Therefore we'll knock.   [*Knocks.*

THE FAIR

> *Guard.* [*Within.*] *Qui est la?*
> *Pucelle. Paisans, pauvres gens de France:*
> Poor market-folks, that come to sell their corn.
> *Guard.* [*Opening the gates.*] Enter, go in; the market-bell is rung.
> *Pucelle.* Now, Rouen, I'll shake thy bulwarks to the ground."

The " market-bell " was rung at the hour when the market was to begin.

In the same play (v. 5. 54), when a dower is proposed for Margaret, who is to marry Henry, Suffolk says :—

> " A dower, my lords! disgrace not so your king,
>   That he should be so abject, base, and poor,
>   To choose for wealth, and not for perfect love.
>   Henry is able to enrich his queen,
>   And not to seek a queen to make him rich :
>   So worthless peasants bargain for their wives,
>   As market-men for oxen, sheep, or horse."

In 2 *Henry VI.* (v. 2. 62), when Cade has said boastingly, " I am able to endure much," Dick makes the comment, aside : " No question of that; for I have seen him whipped three market-days together."

There are many other allusions to markets, market-men, market-maids, etc., in the plays, but these will suffice for illustration here.

The semi-annual Fair was a market on a grander scale. The increased crowd of dealers called for certain police regulations, and these were strictly enforced. The town council appointed to each trade a particular station in the streets. Thus, raw hides were to be exposed for sale in the Rother Market. Sellers of but-

ter, cheese, wick-yarn, and fruits were to set up their
stalls by the cross at the Guild Chapel. A part of the
High Street was assigned to country butchers. Pew-
terers were ordered to "pitch" their wares in Wood
Street, and to pay fourpence a square yard for the
ground they occupied. Salt-wagons, whose owners did
a large business when salted meats formed the staple
supply of food, were permitted to stand about the cross
in the Rother Market. At various points victuallers
could erect booths. These regulations were necessary
to prevent strife concerning locations, and violations
were punished by heavy fines.

Mr. Knight remarks : "At the joyous Fair-season it
would seem that the wealth of a world was emptied into
Stratford ; not only the substantial things, the wine, the
wax, the wheat, the wool, the malt, the cheese, the clothes,
the napery, such as even great lords sent their stew-
ards to the Fairs to buy, but every possible variety of
such trumpery as fills the pedler's pack, — ribbons,
inkles, caddises, coifs, stomachers, pomanders, brooches,
tapes, shoe-ties. Great dealings were there on these
occasions in beeves and horses, tedious chafferings,
stout affirmations, saints profanely invoked to ratify a
bargain. A mighty man rides into the Fair who scat-
ters consternation around. It is the Queen's Pur-
veyor. The best horses are taken up for her Majesty's
use, at her Majesty's price ; and they probably find
their way to the Earl of Leicester's or the Earl of Warwick's stables at a considerable profit to Master Pur-
veyor. The country buyers and sellers look blank ;
but there is no remedy. There is solace, however, if
there is not redress. The ivy-bush is at many a door,
and the sounds of merriment are within, as the ale and

the sack are quaffed to friendly greetings. In the streets there are morris-dancers, the juggler with his ape, and the minstrel with his ballads. We may imagine the foremost in a group of boys listening to the 'small popular musics sung by these *cantabanqui* upon benches and barrels' heads,' or more earnestly to some one of the 'blind harpers, or such-like tavern minstrels, that give a fit of mirth for a groat; their matters being for the most part stories of old time as *The Tale of Sir Topas, Bevis of Southampton, Guy of Warwick, Adam Bell and Clymme of the Clough*, and such other old romances or historical rhymes, made purposely for the recreation of the common people.' A bold fellow, who is full of queer stories and cant phrases, strikes a few notes upon his gittern, and the lads and lasses are around him ready to dance their country measures. . . .

"The Fair is over; the booths are taken down; the woolen statute-caps, which the commonest people refuse to wear because there is a penalty for not wearing them, are packed up again; the prohibited felt hats are all sold; the millinery has found a ready market among the sturdy yeomen, who are careful to propitiate their home-staying wives after the fashion of the Wife of Bath's husbands. . . . The juggler has packed up his cup and balls; the last cudgel-play has been fought out:—

> "'Near the dying of the day
> There will be a cudgel-play,
> Where a coxcomb will be broke
> Ere a good word can be spoke:
> But the anger ends all here,
> Drench'd in ale, or drown'd in beer.'

Morning comes, and Stratford hears only the quiet steps of its native population."

There are many allusions, literal and figurative, to these fairs in Shakespeare's plays, a few of which may be cited here as specimens.

In *Love's Labour 's Lost*, besides the one quoted above (page 199), we find the following simile in Biron's eulogy of Rosaline (iv. 3. 235):—

> "Of all complexions the cull'd soverignty
> Do meet, as at a fair, in her fair cheek."

In the same play (v. 2. 2), the Princess says to her ladies, referring to the presents they have received:—

> "Sweet hearts, we shall be rich ere we depart
> If fairings come thus plentifully in."

It was so common a practice to buy presents at fairs that the word *fairing*, which originally meant presents thus bought, came to be used in a more general sense, as in this passage and many others that might be quoted.

In *The Winter's Tale* (iv. 3. 109) the Clown says of the merry peddler Autolycus that "he haunts wakes, fairs, and bear-baitings." Later (iv. 4) we meet the rogue at the sheep-shearing, where he finds a good market for ribbons, gloves, and other "fairings," which the swains buy for their sweethearts; and when the festival is over he says: "I have sold all my trumpery; not a counterfeit stone, not a ribbon, glass, pomander, brooch, table-book, ballad, knife, tape, glove, shoe-tie, bracelet, horn-ring, to keep my pack from fasting; they throng who should buy first, as if my trinkets had been hallowed and brought a benediction to the buyer."

In 2 *Henry IV.* (iii. 2. 43) Shallow asks his cousin Silence, "How a good yoke of bullocks now at Stamford fair?" and Silence replies, "By my troth, I was not there." Later (v. 1. 26) Davy asks Shallow: "Sir, do you mean to stop any of William's wages, about the sack he lost the other day at Hinckley fair?"

In *Henry VIII.* (v. 4. 73) the Chamberlain, seeing the crowd gathered to get a sight of the royal procession, exclaims :—

"Mercy o' me, what a multitude are here !
They grow still too; from all parts they are coming,
As if we kept a fair here."

In *Lear* (iii 6. 78) Edgar, in his random talk while pretending to be insane, cries: "Come, march to wakes and fairs and market-towns !"

The "wakes," mentioned so often in connection with fairs, were annual feasts kept to commemorate the dedication of a church; called so, as an old writer tells us, "because the night before they were used to watch till morning in the church." The next day was given up to feasting and all sorts of rural merriment. In the churchwardens' accounts of the time we find charges for "wine and sugar," for "bread, wine, and ale," and the like, for "certain of the parish," for "the singing men and singing children," and others, on these occasions.

At these wakes, as at the fairs and other large gatherings, whether festal or commercial, hawkers and peddlers came to sell their wares and merchants set up their stalls and booths, often in the very churchyard

and even on a Sunday. The clergy naturally de-
nounced this profanation of the Sabbath, but it was
not entirely suppressed until the reign of Henry VI.

Stubbes, in his *Anatomy of Abuses* (1583), inveighed
against these wakes, as against the May-day sports
(page 176 above), especially on account of the money
wasted at them, "insomuch as the poor men that bear
the charges of these feasts and wakes are the poorer
and keep the worser houses a long time after: and no
marvel, for many spend more at one of these wakes
than in all the whole year besides."

Herrick, in his *Hesperides* (page 196 above) took a
more cheerful view of such rural holidays :—

> " Come, Anthea, let us two
> Go to feast, as others do.
> Tarts and custards, creams and cakes,
> Are the junkets still at wakes ;
> Unto which the tribes resort,
> Where the business is the sport.
> Morris-dancers thou shalt see,
> Marian too in pageantry ;
> And a mimic to devise
> Many grinning properties.
> Players there will be, and those
> Base in action as in clothes ;
> Yet with strutting they will please
> The incurious villages.
>
> *   *   *   *   *   *
>
> Happy rustics, best content
> With the cheapest merriment ;
> And possess no other fear
> Than to want the wake next year ;"

that is, to miss or lack it.

RURAL OUTINGS.

Much of the recreation, as of the education, of William Shakespeare was in the fields. "He is rarely a descriptive poet, distinctively so called; but images of mead and grove, of dale and upland, of forest depths, of quiet walks by gentle rivers,—reflections of his own native scenery,—spread themselves without an effort over all his writings. All the occupations of a rural life are glanced at or embodied in his characters. He wreathes all the flowers of the field in his delicate chaplets; and even the nicest mysteries of the gardener's art can be expounded by him. His poetry in this, as in all other great essentials, is like the operations of nature itself; we see not its workings. But we may be assured, from the very circumstance of its appearing so accidental, so spontaneous in its relations to all external nature and to the country life, that it had its foundation in very early and very accurate observation. Stratford was especially fitted to have been the 'green lap' in which the boy-poet was 'laid.' The whole face of creation here wore an aspect of quiet loveliness."

The surrounding country was no less beautiful; and William would naturally become familiar with it in his boyish rambles and in his visits to his relatives. The village of Wilmcote, the home of his mother, was within walking distance; and so was Snitterfield, where his father lived before he came to Stratford, and where his uncle Henry still resided. All through the wooded district of Arden the name of Shakespeare was very common, and among those who bore it were probably other families more or less closely related to John Shakespeare's.

However that may have been, the enterprising glover and wool-merchant must have had large dealings with the neighboring farmers; and William must have seen much of rural life and employments in the company of his father, or when wandering at his own free will in the country about Stratford.   In no other way could he have gained the intimate acquaintance with farming and gardening operations of which his works bear evidence.   He went to London before his literary career began, and lived there until it closed, with only brief occasional visits to Warwickshire.   In the metropolis he could not have added much to his early lessons in the country life and character of which he has given us such graphic and faithful delineations.   These are thoroughly fresh and real; they tell of the outdoor life he loved, and never smell of the study-lamp, as Milton's and Spenser's allusions to plants, flowers, and other natural objects often do.

Volumes have been written on the plant-lore and garden-craft of Skakespeare; and the authors dwell equally on the poet's ingrained love of the country and his keen observation of natural phenomena and the agricultural practice of the time.

In *Richard II.* (iii. 4. 29–66) the Gardener and his Servant draw lessons of political wisdom from the details of their occupation :—

" *Gardener.* Go, bind thou up yon dangling apricocks,
Which, like unruly children, make their sire
Stoop with oppression of their prodigal weight;
Give some supportance to the bending twigs.
Go thou, and like an executioner
Cut off the heads of too-fast-growing sprays,
That look too lofty in our commonwealth;

All must be even in our government.
You thus employ'd, I will go root away
The noisome weeds, that without profit suck
The soil's fertility from wholesome flowers.
    Servant. Why should we, in the compass of a pale,
Keep law, and form, and due proportion,
Showing, as in a model, our firm estate,
When our sea-walled garden, the whole land,
Is full of weeds; her fairest flowers chok'd up,
Her fruit-trees all unprun'd, her hedges ruin'd,
Her knots disorder'd, and her wholesome herbs
Swarming with caterpillars?
    Gardener.   Hold thy peace!
He that hath suffer'd this disorder'd spring
Hath now himself met with the fall of leaf.
The weeds that his broad-spreading leaves did shelter,
That seem'd in eating him to hold him up,
Are pluck'd up, root and all, by Bolingbroke;
I mean the Earl of Wiltshire, Bushy, Green.
    Servant. What, are they dead?
    Gardener. They are; and Bolingbroke
Hath seiz'd the wasteful king.—O, what pity is it,
That he hath not so trimm'd and dress'd his land
As we this garden! We at time of year
Do wound the bark, the skin of our fruit-trees,
Lest, being over-proud with sap and blood,
With too much riches it confound itself:
Had he done so to great and growing men,
They might have liv'd to bear, and he to taste
Their fruits of duty. All superfluous branches
We lop away, that bearing boughs may live:
Had he done so, himself had borne the crown,
Which waste of idle hours hath quite thrown down."

Mr. Ellacombe, commenting upon this dialogue, remarks: "This most interesting passage would almost

14

tempt us to say that Shakespeare was a gardener by profession ; certainly no other passages that have been brought to prove his real profession are more minute than this. It proves him to have had practical experience in the work, and I think we may safely say that he was no mere 'prentice hand in the use of the pruning-knife." But this play was written in London, when he could hardly have known anything more of practical gardening than he had learned in his boyhood and youth at Stratford.

Grafting and the various ways of propagating plants by cuttings, slips, etc., are described or alluded to with equal accuracy; also the mischief done by weeds, blights, frosts, and other enemies of the husbandman and horticulturist. He writes on all these matters as we might expect him to have done in his last years at Stratford, after he had had actual experience in the management of a large garden at New Place and in farming operations on other lands he had bought in the neighborhood ; but all these passages, like the one quoted from *Richard II.*, were written long before he had a garden of his own. They were reminiscences of his observation as a boy, not the results of his experience as a country gentleman.

NOTES

ABBREVIATIONS, except a few of the most familiar, have been avoided in the Notes, as in other parts of the book. The references to act, scene, and line in the quotations from Shakespeare are added for the convenience of the reader or student, who may sometimes wish to refer to the context. The line-numbers are those of the "Globe" edition, which vary from those of my edition only in scenes that are wholly or partly in *prose*.

The numbers appended to names of authors (as in the note on page 22, for example) are the dates of their birth and death. An interrogation-mark after a date (as in the note on page 114) indicates that it is uncertain. I have not thought it necessary to insert biographical notes concerning well-known authors, like Spenser, Milton, etc.

NOTES

Page 3.—*Michael Drayton.* He was born in Warwickshire in 1563. Of his personal history very little is known. His most famous work, the *Poly-Olbion* (or *Polyolbion*, as it is often printed), is a poem of about 30,000 lines, the subject of which, as he himself states it, is "a chorographical description of all the tracts, rivers, mountains, forests, and other parts of this renowned Isle of Great Britain ; with intermixture of the most remarkable stories, antiquities, wonders, etc., of the same." His *Ballad of Agincourt* (see *Tales from English History*, p. 39) has been called "the most perfect and patriotic of English ballads." Drayton was made poet-laureate in 1626. He died in 1631, and was buried in Westminster Abbey.

Page 4.—*Her Bear.* The badge of the Earls of Warwick.

Wilmcote. A small village about three miles from Stratford-on-Avon. The name is also written *Wilmecote*, and *Wilnecote ;* and in old documents, *Wilmcott, Wincott*, etc. It is probably the *Wincot* of *The Taming of the Shrew* (ind. 2. 23) and the *Woncot* of 2 *Henry IV.* (v. 1. 42).

Dugdale. Sir William Dugdale (1605–1686), one of the most learned of English antiquaries. His *Antiquities of Warwickshire* (1656) is said to have been the result of twenty years' laborious research.

Page 7.—*Beauchamp.* Pronounced *Beech'-am.*

The herse of brass hoops. The word *herse* (the same as *hearse*) originally meant a harrow ; then a temporary framework, often shaped like a harrow, used for supporting candles at a funeral service, and placed over the coffin ; then a kind of frame or cage over an effigy on a tomb ; and finally a carriage for bearing a corpse to the grave. For the third meaning (which we have here), compare Ben Jonson's *Epitaph on the Countess of Pembroke :*—

> " Underneath this sable herse
> Lies the subject of all verse," etc.

The garter. Showing that he was a Knight of the Garter.

The noble Impe. The word *imp* originally meant a scion, shoot, or slip of a tree or plant ; then, figuratively, human offspring or progeny, as here and in many passages in writers of the time. Holinshed the chronicler speaks of " Prince Edward, that goodlie impe," and Churchyard calls Edward VI. " that impe of grace." Fulwell, addressing Anne Boleyn, refers to Elizabeth as " thy royal impe." As first applied to a young or small devil, the word had this same meaning of offspring, " an imp of Satan " being a child of Satan. How it came later to mean a mischievous urchin I leave the small folk themselves to guess.

Page 10.—*The famous "dun cow."* This, according to the legend, was " a monstrous wild and cruel beast" which ravaged the country about Dunsmore. Guy also slew a wild boar of " passing might and strength," and a dragon " black as any coal" which was long the terror of Northumberland. Compare the old ballad of *Sir Guy :*—

> " On Dunsmore heath I also slew
> A monstrous wild and cruel beast,
> Call'd the Dun-cow of Dunsmore heath,
> Which many people had opprest.

> " Some of her bones in Warwick yet
> Still for a monument do lie ;
> And there exposed to lookers' view
> As wondrous strange they may espy.

> " A dragon in Northumberland
> I also did in fight destroy,
> Which did both man and beast oppress,
> And all the country sore annoy."

Page 13.—*Master Robert Laneham.* He was an English merchant who became "doorkeeper of the council-chamber" to the Earl of Leicester. He wrote an account, in the form of a letter, of the festivities in honor of this visit of Elizabeth to Kenilworth, which was afterwards printed. He is one of the characters in Scott's *Kenilworth.*

Page 14.—*Theatres,* etc. The cut facing page 14 shows one of the movable stages referred to by Dugdale ; also two of "the three tall spires" mentioned by Tennyson in the poem of *Godiva.* The nearer church is St. Michael's, said to be the largest parish church in England, with a steeple 303 feet high. Beyond it is Trinity Church, with a spire 237 feet high.

Page 15. — *The most beautiful in the kingdom.* There is a familiar story of two Englishmen who laid a wager as to which was the finest walk in England. After the money was put up, one named the walk from Stratford to Coventry, and the other that from Coventry to Stratford. How the umpire decided the case is not recorded.

Page 16.—*The Cappers.* The makers of caps.

Page 17.—*King Herod.* Longfellow, in his *Golden Legend,* introduces a miracle-play, *The Nativity,* which is supposed to be acted at Strasburg. Herod figures in it after the blustering fashion of the ancient dramas. Young readers will get a good idea of these plays from this imitation of them.

Page 18.—*Other allusions to these old plays.* See, for instance, *Twelfth Night,* iv. 2. 134, 2 *Henry IV.* iii. 2. 343, *Richard III.* iii. 1. 82, *Hamlet,* iii. 4. 98, etc., and the notes in my edition.

Page 19.—*The legend of Godiva.* See Tennyson's *Godiva.*

Page 22.—*Dr. Forman.* Simon Forman (1552–1611), a noted astrologer and quack, who wrote several books, and left a diary, in which he describes at considerable length the plot of Shakespeare's *Macbeth,* which he saw performed "at the Globe, 1610, the 20th of April, Saturday." See my edition of *Macbeth,* p. 9.

Page 23.—The head of Sir Thomas Lucy is from his monument in Charlecote church.

Page 24.—*A willow grows aslant a brook.* See *Hamlet,* iv. 7. 165. Some editions of Shakespeare follow the reading of the early quartos, "ascaunt the brook," which means the same. This willow (the *Salix alba*) grows on the banks of the Avon, and from the looseness of the soil the trees often partly lose their hold, and bend "aslant" the stream.

Page 26.—*The banished Duke in As You Like It, etc.* See the play, ii. 1. 1–18.

His maidens ever sing of "blue-veined violets," etc. The "blue-vein'd violets" are mentioned in *Venus and Adonis*, 125 ; the "daisies pied" (variegated), and the "lady-smocks all silver-white," in *Love's Labour's Lost*, v. 2. 904, 905 ; and the "pansies" in *Hamlet*, iv. 5. 176.

Page 27.—*A manor of the Bishop of Worcester.* Under the feudal system, a *manor* was a landed estate, with a village or villages upon it the inhabitants of which were generally *villeins*, or serfs of the owner or lord. These *villeins* were either *regardant* or *in gross.* The former "belonged to the manor as fixtures, passing with it when it was conveyed or inherited, and they could not be sold or transferred as persons separate from the land"; the latter "belonged personally to their lord, who could sell or transfer them at will." The *bordarii, bordars,* or *cottagers,* "seem to have been distinguished from the *villeins* simply by their smaller holdings." For the menial services rendered by the villeins, and their condition generally, see the following pages.

Page 32.—*A chantry.* A church or a chapel (as here) endowed with lands or other revenues for the maintenance of one or more priests to sing or say mass daily for the soul of the donor or the souls of persons named by him. Cf. *Henry V.* iv. 1. 318 :—

> "I have built
> Two chantries, where the sad and solemn priests
> Sing still for Richard's soul."

Page 40.—*Present her at the leet, etc.* Complain of her for using common stone jugs instead of the quart-pots duly sealed or stamped as being of legal size.

A substantial ducking-stool, etc. The *ducking-stool* was kept up as a punishment for scolds in some parts of England until late in the 18th century. An antiquary, writing about 1780, tells of seeing it used at Magdalen bridge in Cambridge. He says : "The chair hung by a pulley fastened to a beam about the middle of the bridge ; and the woman having been fastened in the chair, she was let under water three times successively, and then taken out. . . . The ducking-stool was constantly hanging in its place, and on the back panel of it was an engraving representing devils laying hold of scolds. Some time after, a new chair was erected in the place of the old one, having the same device carved on it, and well painted and ornamented."

Page 41.—*Butts.* Places for the practice of archery, the *butts* being properly the targets.

Page 45.—*Pinfold.* Shakespeare uses the word in *The Two Gentlemen of Verona* (i. 1. 114): "I mean the pound—a pinfold"; and in *Lear* (ii. 2. 9): "in Lipsbury pinfold." It was so called because stray beasts were *pinned* or shut up in it.

Page 46.—*One wagon tract.* That is, track. *Tract* in this sense is obsolete.

Page 49.—*In which William Shakespeare was probably born.* We have no positive information on this point; but we know that John Shakespeare resided in Henley Street in 1552, and that he became the owner of this house at some time before 1590. The tradition that this was the poet's birthplace is ancient and has never been disproved. Mr. Halliwell-Phillipps, one of the most careful and conservative of critics, says: "There can be no doubt that from the earliest period at which we have, or are likely to have, a record of the fact, it was the tradition of Stratford that the birthplace is correctly so designated"; and he himself accepts the tradition as almost certainly founded upon fact.

The cut facing page 50, like that facing page 56, gives an idea of the interior appearance of these old houses. The room in which tradition says that Shakespeare was born is the front room on the second floor (what English people call the "first floor"), at the left-hand side of the house as seen in the cut on page 49.

In the other cut (the interior of the cottage in which Anne Hathaway, whom Shakespeare married, is said to have lived at Shottery) the very large old-fashioned fire-place is to be noted. Persons could actually sit "in the chimney corner," like the woman in the picture. The grate is a modern addition.

Page 51.—*New Place.* Sir Hugh Clopton, for whom this mansion was erected, speaks of it in 1496 as his "great house," a title by which it was commonly known at Stratford for more than two centuries. Shakespeare bought it in 1597 for £60, a moderate price for so large a property; but in a document of the time of Edward VI. it is described as having been for some time "in great ruin and decay and unrepaired," and it was probably in a dilapidated condition when it was transferred to Shakespeare. It had been sold by the Clopton family in 1563, and in 1567 came into the possession of William Underhill, whose family continued to hold it until Shakespeare bought it. He left it by his will to his daughter Susanna, who had married Dr. John Hall, and who probably occupied it until her death in 1649, when she had been a widow for fourteen years. The estate descended to her daughter Elizabeth, who was first married to Thomas Nash, and afterwards to Sir Thomas Barnard. In 1675 it was sold again, but ultimately reverted by will to the Clopton family. Sir John Clopton rebuilt the house early in the next century, and it was subsequently occupied by another Hugh Clopton. He died in 1751, and in 1756 the estate was sold to Rev. Francis Gastrell, who pulled the house down in 1759, on account of a quarrel with the town authorities concerning the taxes levied upon it. The year before (1758) he had cut down Shakespeare's mulberry-tree, in order, as tradition says, to save himself the trouble of showing it to visitors. The Stratford people were indignant at this act of vandalism. Mr. Halliwell-Phillipps says that an old inhabitant of the town told him that his father, when a boy, "assisted in breaking Gastrell's windows in revenge for the fall of the tree." It is possible, however, that some injustice has been done the reverend gentleman. Davies, in his *Life of Garrick* (1780), asserts that Gastrell disliked the tree "because it overshadowed his window, and rendered the house, as he thought, subject to damps and moisture." There is also some evidence that the trunk of the tree, which was now a hundred and fifty years old and grown to a great size, had begun to decay. That Gastrell was not indifferent to the poetical associations of the tree is evident from the fact that he kept relics of it, his widow having presented one to the Lichfield Museum in 1778. It is described in a catalogue (1786) of the museum as "an horizontal section of the stock of the mulberry-tree planted by Shakespeare at Stratford-upon-Avon."

Page 52.— *William Harrison.* An English clergyman, of whose history we know little except that he was born in London, became rector of Radwinter, Essex, and canon of Windsor, wrote a *Description of Britaine and England* and other historical books, and probably died in 1592. His detailed account of the state of England and the manners and customs of the people in the 16th century is particularly valuable.

Page 54.— *Strewn with rushes.* There are many allusions to this in Shakespeare. In *The Taming of the Shrew* (iv. 1. 48), when Petruchio is coming home, Grumio asks : "Is supper ready, the house trimmed, rushes strewed, cobwebs swept ?" Compare *Romeo and Juliet*, i. 4. 36 : "Tickle the senseless rushes with their heels" (that is, in dancing) ; *Cymbeline*, ii. 2. 13 :—

> "Our Tarquin thus
> Did softly press the rushes," etc.

Page 55. — *Thomas Coryat*, born in 1577 and educated at Oxford, was celebrated for his pedestrian journeys on the Continent of Europe. In 1608 he travelled through France, Germany, and Italy, "walking 1975 miles, more than half of which were accomplished in one pair of shoes, which were only once mended, and on his return were hung up in the Church of Odcombe." Of this tour he wrote an account entitled "Coryat's Crudities hastily gobled up in five months' Travels in France," etc. He died at Surat in 1617, after explorations in Greece, Egypt, and India.

Page 56. — *Bullein*. William Bullein, or Bulleyn, born about 1500, was a learned physician and botanist. His *Government of Health* was very popular in its day. He wrote several other books of medicine. He died in 1576.

Page 57. — *His Anatomy of Melancholy*. Of this famous work, written by Robert Burton (1577–1640), Dr. Johnson said that it was "the only book that ever took me out of bed two hours sooner than I wished to rise."

Page 60. — *Francis Seager*. Of his personal history, as of that of *Hugh Rhodes*, nothing of importance is known.

Page 61. — *He is then to make low curtsy*. This form of obeisance was used by both sexes in Shakespeare's day. Cf. 2 *Henry IV*. ii. 1. 135 : "if a man will make courtesy and say nothing, he is virtuous"; and the epilogue to the same play : "First my fear, then my courtesy, last my speech." *Curtsy* is a modern spelling of the word in this sense.

Page 62. — *Caraways*. The word occurs once in Shakespeare (2 *Henry IV*. v. 3. 3 : "a dish of caraways"), where it probably has the same meaning as here ; but some have thought that the reference is to a variety of apple.

Page 63. — *Treatably*. Tractably, smoothly. Cf. Marston, *What You Will*, ii. 1 : "Not too fast ; say [recite] treatably."

Much forder. We find *d* and *th* used interchangeably in many words in old writers ; as *fadom* and *fathom*, *murder* and *murther*, etc.

Page 64. — *To charge thee with than*. We find *than* for *then* in Shakespeare, *Lucrece*, 1440 :—

> " To Simois' reedy banks the red blood ran,
> Whose waves to imitate the battle sought
> With swelling ridges; and their ranks began
> To break upon the galled shore, and than
> Retire again," etc.

Here, it will be seen, the word rhymes with *ran* and *began*. On the other hand, *than* in the early eds. of Shakespeare and other writers of the time is generally *then*.

Page 65.— *Utterly detest.* That is, *detested.* The omission of *-ed* in the participles of verbs ending in *d* and *t* (or *te*) was formerly not uncommon in prose as well as poetry. Cf. Bacon, *Essay* 16 : "Their means are less exhaust"; and *Essay* 38 : "They have degenerate." See also *Richard III.* iii. 7. 179 : "For first was he contract to Lady Lucy," etc.

Page 66.— *To enter children.* To begin their training. The word is now obsolete in this sense of introducing to, or initiating into, anything. Cf. Ben Jonson, *Epicœne*, iii. 1 : "I am bold to enter these gentlemen in your acquaintance"; Walton, *Complete Angler :* "to enter you into the art of fishing," etc.

Thorow. Thorough and *through* were originally the same word, and we find them and their derivatives used interchangeably in Shakespeare and other old writers. Cf. *A Midsummer-Night's Dream*, ii. 1. 3 :—

> "Over hill, over dale,
> Thorough bush, thorough brier,
> Over park, over pale,
> Thorough flood, thorough fire."

So we find *thoroughly* and *throughly* (*Hamlet*, iv. 5. 36, etc.), *thoroughfares* and *throughfares* (*Merchant of Venice*, ii. 7. 42, etc.).

Page 67.— *The Ship of Fools.* A translation (with original modifications) of the *Narrenschiff* of Sebastian Brandt (or Brant), a German satire (1494) upon the follies of different classes of men. It was made in 1508 by Alexander Barclay, who died at an advanced age in 1552. He was educated at Oxford, became a priest, and was vicar of several parishes in England before he was promoted to that of All Saints, Lombard Street, London, a few weeks previous to his death. *The Ship of Fools* was the first English book in which any mention is made of the New World.

Strutt. Joseph Strutt (1742–1802) was an eminent English antiquarian, who wrote several valuable works in that line of literature and others. The first edition of his *Sports and Pastimes of the People of England* appeared in 1801.

Page 69.— *Taylor the Water-Poet.* John Taylor (1580–1654), a waterman who afterwards became a collector of wine duties in London. He wrote much in prose and verse, and was very popular in his day.

Page 70.— *Dr. John Jones.* A physician, who practised at Bath and Buxton, England, and wrote a number of medical works between 1556 and 1579.

Page 71.—*No other clear allusion to the game, etc.* Some critics have thought there may be a punning allusion to the *stale-mate* of chess in *The Taming of the Shrew,* i. 1. 58 : " To make a stale of me among these mates"; but this is doubtful.

Page 73.—*She was pinch'd.* The *she* is used in a demonstrative sense, referring to one of the company (this maid), as *he* (that man) is in the next line. The *Friar* is the Friar Rush of the fairy mythology, whom Milton seems here to identify with Jack-o'-the-Lantern, or Will-o'-the- Wisp, the luminous appearance sometimes seen in marshy places ; but Friar Rush, according to Keightley, " haunted houses, not fields, and was never the same with Jack-o'-the-Lantern."

Page 74.—*The drudging goblin.* Robin Goodfellow, the Puck of Shakespeare. Cf. *A Midsummer-Night's Dream,* ii, 1. 40 :—

> " They that Hobgoblin call you and sweet Puck,
> You do their work, and they shall have good luck."

To bed they creep. Somewhat reluctantly and timidly after the stories of fairies and goblins.

Charles Knight. An English publisher and author (1791–1873), one of the leading editors and biographers of Shakespeare.

Page 75.— *William Painter.* He was born in England about 1537, and died about 1594. He studied at Cambridge in 1554, and in 1561 was made clerk of the ordnance in the Tower of London. In 1566 he published the first volume of *The Palace of Pleasure,* containing sixty tales from Latin, French, and Italian authors. The second volume (1567) contained thirty-four tales. In later editions six more were added, making a hundred in all. The collection is the source from which Shakespeare and other Elizabethan dramatists drew many of their plots.

Page 76.—*Giletta of Narbonne.* The story dramatized by Shakespeare in *All 's Well that Ends Well.*

Page 77.—*The " Gesta Romanorum."* A popular collection of stories in Latin, compiled late in the 13th or early in the 14th century, and often reprinted and translated. The two stories (of the caskets and of the bond) combined in the *Merchant of Venice* are found in it ; and also the story of Theodosius and his daughters, which is like that of *Lear,* though Shakespeare did not take the plot of that tragedy directly from it.

Page 78.—*The trumpet to the morn.* The *trumpeter* that announces the coming of day. *Trumpet* in this sense occurs several times in Shakespeare ; as in *Henry V.* iv. 2. 61 : " I will the banner from a trumpet take," etc.

Extravagant and erring. Both words are used in their etymological sense of wandering. *Extravagant* is, literally, *wandering beyond* (its proper *confine*, or limit).

Arden. There was a Forest of Arden in Warwickshire as well as on the Continent in the northeastern part of France. Drayton, in his *Matilda* (1594), speaks of " Sweet Arden's nightingales," etc.

The ringlets of their dance. The " fairy rings," so called, which were supposed to be made by their dancing on the grass. In *The Tempest* (v. 1. 37) Prospero refers to them thus, in his apostrophe to the various classes of spirits over whom he has control :—

> " You demi-puppets that
> By moonshine do the green sour ringlets make
> Whereof the ewe not bites."

Dr. Grey, in his *Notes on Shakespeare*, says that they are " higher, sourer, and of a deeper green than the grass which grows round them." They were long a mystery even to scientific men, but are now known to be due to the spreading of a kind of *agaricum*, or fungus, which enriches the ground by its decay.

Who tasted the honey-bag of the bee, etc. All these allusions to the fairies are suggested by passages in *A Midsummer-Night's Dream.* The *cankers* are canker-worms, as often in Shakespeare.

Page 79.—*A laund.* An open space in a forest. See 3 *Henry VI.* iii. 1. 2 : " For through this laund anon the deer will come," etc. *Lawn* is a corruption of *laund.*

Page 80. — *Who had command over the spirits, etc.* Like Prospero in *The Tempest.*

Vervain and dill. These were among the plants supposed to be used by witches in their charms ; but many such plants were also believed to be efficacious as counter-charms, or means of protection against witchcraft. *Vervain* was called " the enchanter's plant," on account of its magic potency ; but Aubrey says that it " hinders witches from their wills," and Drayton refers to it as " 'gainst witchcraft much availing."

Page 81.—The ancient font represented in the cut was in use in the Stratford Church until about the middle of the 17th century. Shakespeare was doubtless baptized at it.

Page 82.—*John Stow.* A noted English antiquarian and historian (1525–1604). His *Survey of London* (1598) is the standard authority on old London.

Page 83.—*The calendars of their nativity.* Referring to the twin Dromios, who were born at the same time with the twin children of the Abbess, who is really Emilia, the long-lost wife of Egeus. By a similar figure Antipholus of Syracuse (i. 2. 41) says of Dromio, " Here comes the almanac of my true date."

Caraways. See on page 62 above. *Marmalet* is an obsolete form of *marmalade.* *Marchpane* was a kind of almond-cake, much esteemed in the time of Shakespeare. Compare *Romeo and Juliet,* i. 5. 9 : " Good thou, save me a piece of marchpane." *Sweet-suckers* are dried sweetmeats or sugar-plums, also called *suckets, succades,* etc.

Page 85.—*Wote.* Know ; more commonly written *wot.* It is the first and third persons singular, indicative present, of the obsolete verb *wit. Unweeting (unwitting),* unknowing or unconscious, is from the same verb.

Page 86.—*Thomas Lupton.* He wrote several books besides his *Thousand Notable Things,* which was a collection of medical recipes, stories, etc. Little is known of his personal history.

Robert Heron. He was a Scotchman (1764–1807), who wrote books of travel, geography, history, etc.

Warlocks. Persons supposed to be in league with the devil ; sorcerers or wizards.

Page 87.—*Beshrew.* Originally a mild imprecation of evil, but often used playfully, as here. Compare the similar modern use of *confound,* which originally meant ruin or destroy ; as in the *Merchant of Venice,* iii. 2. 271 : " So keen and greedy to confound a man," etc.

Page 88.—*Astrologaster.* The full title was " The Astrologaster, or the Figurecaster : Rather the Arraignment of Artless Astrologers and Fortune Tellers."

Page 89.—*In the following form.* There were other forms, but this was regarded as one of the most potent. It will be seen that the word, as here arranged, can be read in various ways ; as, for instance, following each line to the end and then up the right-hand side of the triangle, etc. An old writer, after giving directions to write the word in this triangular form, adds : " Fold the paper so as to conceal the writing, and stitch it into the form of a cross with white thread. This amulet wear in the bosom, suspended by a linen ribbon, for nine days. Then go in dead silence, before sunrise, to the bank of a stream that flows eastward, take the amulet from off the neck, and fling it backwards into the water. If you open or read it, the charm is destroyed." It was thought to be efficacious for the cure of fevers, "especially quartan and semi-tertian agues."

Thomas Lodge. He was born about 1556, and died in 1625, and wrote plays, novels, songs, translations, etc. His *Rosalynde* (1590) furnished Shakespeare with the plot of *As You Like It.*

Page 90.—*Robert Greene* (1560–1592) was a popular dramatist, novelist, and poet in his day. In his *Groatsworth of Wit* (published in 1592, after his death) he attacked the rising Shakespeare as "an upstart crow," who was "in his own conceit the only Shake-scene in a country." Shakespeare afterwards took the story of *The Winter's Tale* from Greene's *Pandosto*, or *Dorastus and Fawnia*, as it was subsequently entitled.

Webster's White Devil. John Webster, who wrote in the early part of the 17th century, was a dramatist noted for his tragedies, among which *The White Devil* (1612) is reckoned one of the best. Of his biography nothing worth mentioning is known.

Burton, in his Anatomy of Melancholy. See on page 57 above.

Reginald Scot, who died in 1599, is chiefly known by his *Discoverie of Witchcraft,* the main facts concerning which are given here.

Page 91.—*Wierus.* The Latin form of the name of *Weier,* a German physician, who in 1563 published a book (*De Præstigiis Demonum*) in which the general belief in magic and witchcraft was attacked.

We infer that Shakespeare had read Scot's book. However this may be, we are sure that he had read a book by Dr. Samuel Harsnet (1561–1631) entitled *Declaration of Egregious Popish Impostures, etc., under the pretence of casting out devils* (1603), from which he took the names of some of the devils in *Lear* (iii. 4).

Page 96.—*Henry Peacham.* "A travelling tutor, musician, painter, and author," who wrote on drawing and painting, etiquette, education, etc. His father, whose name was the same, was also an author, and it is doubtful whether certain books were written by him or by his son.

Roger Ascham (1515–1568) was a noted classical scholar and author. He was tutor to Elizabeth (1548–1550), and Latin Secretary to Mary and Elizabeth (1553–1568). His chief works were the *Toxophilus* (1545) and the *Scholemaster* (see page 115 below).

Page 97.—*Took on him as a conjurer.* Pretended to be a conjurer. Compare 2 *Henry IV.* iv. 1. 60 : "I take not on me here as a physician."

Page 98.—*Who could speak Latin, etc.* Latin, the language of the church, was used in exorcising spirits. Compare *Hamlet* (i. 1. 42), where, on the appearance of the Ghost, Marcellus says : "Thou art a scholar; speak to it, Horatio." So in *Much Ado About Nothing* (ii. 1. 264), Benedick, after comparing Beatrice to "the infernal Ate," adds : "I would to God some scholar would conjure her !" See also Beaumont and Fletcher, *The Night - Walker,* ii. 1:—

> "Let 's call the butler up, for he speaks Latin,
> And that will daunt the devil."

Page 99.—*Transparent horn.* Used to protect the paper, as explained in the quotation from Shenstone on page 101. The horn-book was really "of stature small," the figure on page 100 being of the exact size of the specimen described. One delineated by Mr. Halliwell-Phillipps is of about the same size. See Chambers's *Book of Days,* vol. i. p. 46.

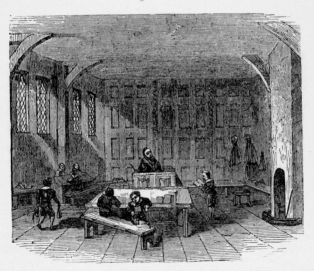

INTERIOR OF GRAMMAR SCHOOL, BEFORE THE RESTORATION

Page 101.—*Shenstone.* William Shenstone (1714–1763) was educated at Pembroke College, Oxford. His best-known work is *The Schoolmistress.*

Page 102.—*The modern plastered ceiling, etc.* This has been removed within the past few years. Its appearance before the restoration is shown in the cut (from Knight's *Biography of Shakspere*).

Page 103.—*Sententiæ Pueriles.* Literally, Boyish Sentences, or Sentences for Boys.

Sir Hugh Evans. The title of *Sir* (equivalent to the Latin *dominus*) was given to priests. The "hedge-priest" in *As You Like It* (iii. 3) is called "Sir Oliver Martext." In *Twelfth Night* (iii. 4. 298) Viola says: "I had rather go with sir priest than sir knight."

'Od's nouns. Probably a corruption of "God's wounds," which is also contracted into *Swounds* and *Zounds.* So we find "od's heartlings," "od's pity," etc. Dame Quickly confounds *'od* and *odd.*

Page 104.—*Articles.* Sir Hugh uses the word in the sense of "demonstratives." This shows that the *Accidence* mentioned above as the book from which Shakespeare got his first lessons in Latin (as Halliwell-Phillipps and other authorities state) gave some of the elementary facts in precisely the same form in which they appear in the Latin Grammar written *in English* and published in 1574 with the title, "A Short Introduction of Grammar, generally to be used : compiled and set forth for the bringing up of all those that intend to attaine to the knowledge of the Latine Tongue." I transcribe this from the edition published at Oxford in 1651 (a copy in the Harvard University library, which appears to be the one studied by President Ezra Stiles when he was a boy). In this book (page 3), under the head of "Articles," we read :—

"Articles are borrowed of the Pronoune, and be thus declined :

Singulariter.	Nomin. hic, hæc, hoc. Genetivo hujus. Dativo huic. Acc. hunc, hanc, hoc. Vocativo caret. Ablativo hoc, hac, hoc.	Pluraliter.	Nomin. hi, hæ, hæc. Gen. horum, harum, horum. Dativo his. Accus. hos, has, hæc. Vocativo caret. Ablativo his."

It will be noticed that the names of the cases are in Latin, as in Shakespeare. He may have used this very grammar.

Hang-hog is Latin for Bacon. Suggested by the hanging up of the pork during the process of curing. There is an old story of Sir Nicholas Bacon (father of the philosopher), who was a judge. A criminal whom he was about to sentence begged mercy on account of kinship. " Prithee, said my lord, how came that in ? Why, if it please you, my lord, your name is *Bacon* and mine is *Hog*, and in all ages Hog and Bacon are so near kindred that they are not to be separated. Ay, but, replied the judge, you and I cannot be of kindred unless you be hanged ; for Hog is not Bacon till it be well hanged."

Leave your prabbles. That is, your *brabbles.* The word literally means quarrels or broils ; as in *Twelfth Night,* v. 1. 68 : " In private brabble did we apprehend him." Sir Hugh uses it loosely with reference to the Dame's interruptions and criticisms.

O !—vocativo, O ! The boy hesitates, trying to recall the vocative, but Sir Hugh reminds him that it is wanting—*caret* in Latin, which suggests *carrot* to the Dame. The *O* is suggested by its use before the vocative case of nouns in the paradigms in the *Accidence,* which probably here also agrees with the *Short Introduction,* where in the first declension we find : " *Vocativo ô musa*"; in the second : " *Vocativo ô magister,*" etc.

William Lilly (or Lily), the author of the Latin Grammar mentioned on page 105, was born about 1468 and died in 1523. He was an eminent scholar and the first master of St. Paul's School, London. His Grammar (written in Latin) was entitled " Brevissima Institutio, seu, Ratio Grammatices cognoscendæ, ad omnium puerorum utilitatem præscripta." Of this book more than three hundred editions were printed, the latest mentioned by Allibone (who, by the way, gives the title of the Grammar in an imperfect and ungrammatical form) having been issued in 1817. A copy of the 1651 edition is bound with the *Short Introduction* of the same date in the Harvard Library. Lilly was the author of both.

You must be preeches. That is, you must be *breeched,* or flogged. Compare *The Taming of the Shrew* (iii. i. 18), where Bianca says to her teachers : " I am no breeching scholar in the schools."

Sprag. That is, *sprack,* which meant quick, ready. The word is Scotch, as well as Provincial English, and Scott uses it in *Waverley* (chap. xliii.) : " all this fine sprack [lively] festivity and jocularity."

Page 105.—*A passage from Terence.* In the play, as in the Grammar, it reads : " Redime te captum quam queas minimo." The original Latin is : " Quid agas, nisi ut te redimas captum," etc.

Page 106.—*Richard Mulcaster.* The poet Spenser was one of his pupils at Merchant-Taylors School in 1568 see (Church's *Spenser* in "English Men of Letters" series). In 1596 Mulcaster became master of St. Paul's School. He died in 1611. The title of the book quoted here was *The First Part of the Elementarie . . . of the Right Writing of our English Tung*. The author's theory was better than his practice, as the specimen of his "right writing" given here will suffice to show. It is to be hoped that his oral style was less clumsy and involved.

Correctors for the print. Whether this refers to persons correcting manuscript for the press or to proof-readers is doubtful, but probably the former. Some have denied that there was any proof-reading in the Elizabethan age; but variations in copies of the same edition of a book (the First Folio of Shakespeare, published in 1623, for instance) prove that corrections in the text were sometimes made even after the printing had begun. The author also sometimes did some proof-reading. At the end of Beeton's *Will of Wit* (1599) we find this note: "What faults are escaped in the printing, finde by discretion, and excuse the author, by other worke that let [hindered] him from attendance to the presse."

Rip up. That is, analyze.

Page 107.—*The natural English.* That is, natives of England.

Will not yield flat to theirs. Will not conform exactly to theirs.

Page 108.—*Bewrayeth.* Shows, makes known. Cf. *Proverbs*, xxvii. 16; *Matthew*, xxvi. 73.

Enfranchisement. This evidently refers to the "naturalization" of foreign words taken into the language, or making their orthography conform to English usage.

Prerogative, etc. This paragraph is somewhat obscure at first reading; but it appears to mean that *common use*, or established usage, settles certain questions concerning which there might otherwise be some doubt.

Likes the pen. Suits the pen. Compare *Hamlet* ii. 2. 80: "it likes us well"; *Henry V.* iii. prol. 32: "The offer likes not," etc.

Particularities. Peculiarities.

Which either cannot understand, etc. The relative is equivalent to *who*, and refers to the preceding *many*. This use of *which* was common in Shakespeare's day. Compare *The Tempest*, iii. 1. 6: "The mistress which I serve," etc.

Or cannot entend to understand, etc. That is, cannot *intend* (of which *entend* is an obsolete form), but the word is here used in a sense which is not recognized in the dictionaries. The meaning seems to be that these "plain people" cannot understand a rule either at sight or after some effort to comprehend it, having neither the *time* nor the *conceit* (intellect) to master it. *Conceit* in this sense is common in Shakespeare and his contemporaries. Compare 2 *Henry IV.* ii. 4. 263: "He a good wit? . . . there's no more conceit in him than is in a mallet."

Page 109. — *John Brinsley* became master of the grammar school at Ashby-de-la-Zouche in 1601, where he remained for sixteen years. The full title of his book is *Ludus Literarius, or the Grammar Schoole* (1612). He writes much better English than Mulcaster, and young people will find no difficulty in understanding the passage quoted from him.

Proceed in learning. That is, pursue their studies after leaving the grammar school.

Page 110. — *Present correction.* Immediate correction, or punishment. For this old sense of *present*, compare 2 *Henry IV.* iv. 3. 80 :—

> "Send Colevile with his confederates
> To York, to present execution."

Countervail. Counterbalance, make up for.

Page 112. — *Willis.* All that is known of this "R. Willis" is from his autobiography, the title of which is, "Mount Tabor, or Private Exercises of a Penitent Sinner, published in the yeare of his age 75, anno Dom. 1639." He is the same person who is quoted on page 161 below.

Page 113. — *His references to schoolboys, etc.* Perhaps we ought not to lay much stress on these. The description of "the whining schoolboy" is from the "Seven Ages" of the cynical Jaques, who describes all these stages of human life in sneering and disparaging terms ; and the other passages simply refer to the proverbial dislike of boys to go to school.

Page 114. — *Thomas Tusser* (1527? — 1580?) was a poet and writer on agriculture. Besides his *One Hundred Points of Good Husbandry* (1557), he wrote *Five Hundred Points of Good Husbandry, United to as Many of Good Wiferie* (1570), etc. He was educated at Oxford, spent ten years at court, and then settled on a farm, where the rest of his life was passed.

Page 115. — *In few of Shakespeare's references to school life, etc.* See on *You must be preeches*, page 227 above ; and compare *Much Ado About Nothing*, ii. 1. 228 :—

> "*Don Pedro.* To be whipped? What's his fault?
> *Benedick.* The flat transgression of a schoolboy," etc.

Page 118.—*A sanctuary against fear.* The allusion is to those sacred places in which criminals could take refuge and be exempt from arrest. There was such a sanctuary within the precincts of Westminster Abbey, which retained its privileges until the dissolution of the monastery, and for debtors until 1602. Compare *Richard III.* (ii. 4. 66), where Queen Elizabeth says : "Come, come, my boy ; we will to sanctuary."

Page 122.—*Hoodman-blind.* In *All 's Well that Ends Well* (iv. 3. 136), when Parolles is brought in blindfolded to his companions in arms, whom he supposes to be enemies that have captured him, one of them says aside, "Hoodman comes."

Loggats. When I was at Amherst College, forty or more years ago, we had this same exercise under the name of "loggerheads"; but I have not seen it or heard of it anywhere else.

Page 125.—*The spirited description of the horse.* Compare page 147 below, where it is quoted at length.

Page 126.—*Alexander Barclay.* See on page 67 above.

Edmund Waller (1605–1687) was an English poet, who was a leader in the Long Parliament, afterwards exiled for being concerned in Royalist plots, returned to England under Cromwell, and was a favorite at court after the Reformation.

Page 127.—*The caitch. Catch* was another name for tennis. *Palle-malle,* or *pall-mall* (pronounced pel-mel'), was a game in which a wooden ball was struck with a mallet, to drive it through a raised iron ring at the end of an alley. It was formerly played in St. James's Park, London, and gave its name to the street known as Pall Mall.

Bishop Butler. Joseph Butler (1692–1752), bishop of Bristol and afterwards of Durham, and author of the famous *Analogy of Religion, etc.* (1736).

Gifford. William Gifford (1757–1826), an English critic and satirical poet, editor of the *Quarterly Review* from 1809 to 1824.

Page 130.—*Mulcaster.* See on page 106 above.

Page 132.—*At Kenilworth in* 1575. See page 12 above.

Page 134.—*A certain place in Cheshire.* The story is told of Congleton in that county, but it is denied by the modern inhabitants. The other place referred to is Ecclesfield in Yorkshire, and I do not know that the statement concerning the pawning of the Bible has been disputed.

Page 135.—*Paris-garden.* It is mentioned in *Henry VIII.* (v. 4. 2), where the Porter of the Palace Yard says to the crowd : "You'll leave your noise anon, ye rascals ! do you take the court for Parish-garden ?" This was a vulgar pronunciation of *Paris-garden*. The place was noted for its noise and disorder.

Page 136.—*Dean Colet.* John Colet (1456–1519), dean of St. Paul's in 1505. The school was founded in 1512.

Page 138.—*Sir Thomas More.* The well-known English author and statesman, born in 1478, and executed on Tower Hill in 1535.

No planets strike. That is, exert a baleful influence ; an allusion to astrology.

No fairy takes. Blasts, or bewitches. Compare *The Merry Wives of Windsor*, iv. 4. 32 : "blasts the tree and takes the cattle," etc.

Page 140.—*It irks me.* It is *irksome* to me, troubles me.

Fool was sometimes used as a term of endearment or pity. Compare *The Winter's Tale* (ii. 1. 18), where Hermione says to her women who are grieved at the unjust charge against her, "Do not weep, poor fools !"

The *forked heads* are heads of arrows. Ascham refers to such in his *Toxophilus*.

Page 141.—*A poor sequester'd stag.* Separated from his companions.

Page 145.—*Professor Baynes.* Thomas Spencer Baynes (1823–1887), professor of English Literature at the University of St. Andrews, Scotland, and editor of the ninth edition of the *Encyclopædia Britannica*.

Page 146.—*The vaward of the day.* The *vanguard*, or early part of the day. Compare *Coriolanus*, i. 6. 53 : "Their bands i' the vaward," etc.

Such gallant chiding. The verb *chide* often meant "to make an incessant noise." Compare *As You Like It*, ii. 1. 7 : "And churlish chiding of the winter's wind " ; *Henry VIII.* iii. 2. 197 : "As doth a rock against the chiding flood," etc.

So flew'd, so sanded. Having the same large hanging chaps and the same sandy color.

Like bells. That is, like a chime of bells.

Tender well. Take good care of.

Emboss'd was a hunter's term for foaming at the mouth in consequence of hard running.

Brach. The word properly meant a female hound, but came to be applied to a particular kind of scenting-dog.

Page 147.—*In the coldest fault.* When the scent was coldest (or faintest), and the hounds most at fault. Compare the quotation from *Venus and Adonis*, page 150 below: "the cold fault."

He cried upon it at the merest loss. He gave the cry when the scent seemed utterly lost. See the passage just referred to. *Mere* was formerly used in the sense of absolute or complete. Compare *Othello*, ii. 2. 3: "the mere perdition of the Turkish fleet" (its entire destruction); *Henry VIII*. iii. 2. 329: "the mere undoing of the kingdom" (its utter ruin), etc.

A youthful Work of Shakespeare's. It was first published in 1593, when he was twenty-nine years of age; and some critics believe that it was written several years earlier, perhaps before he went to London.

Page 148.—*Glisters.* Glistens. Both Shakespeare and Milton use *glister* several times, *glisten* not at all.

Told the steps. Counted them. Compare *The Winter's Tale*, iv. 4. 185: "He sings several tunes faster than you'll tell money." The *teller* in a bank is so called because he does this.

Page 149.—*The hairs, who wave,* etc. *Who* was often used where we should use *which*, and *which* (see on page 108 above) where we should use *who*.

It yearn'd my heart. That is, grieved it. Compare *Henry V.* iv. 3. 26: "It yearns me not when men my garments wear," etc.

Page 150.—*Jauncing.* Riding hard.

Musits. Holes (in fence or hedge) for creeping through. The word, also spelled *muset*, is a diminutive of the obsolete *muse*, which means the same. *Amaze* here means bewilder.

Wat. A familiar name for a hare, as *Reynard* for a fox, etc.

Page 151.—*Mr. John R. Wise.* Compare page 26 above.

Page 155.—The cut is a fac-simile of one in *The Booke of Falconrie* (1575), by George Turbervile, or Turberville (1520?–1595?), an English poet, translator, and writer on hunting, hawking, etc.

Page 156.—*Cotgrave.* Randle Cotgrave, an English lexicographer, who died about 1634. His *French-English Dictionary* (first published in 1611) is still valuable in the study of French and English philology.

Page 159.—*John Skelton.* An English scholar and poet, a protégé of Henry VII. and the tutor of Henry VIII. He was born about 1460, and probably died in 1529. "His rough wit and eccentric character made him the hero of a book of 'merry tales.'"

Page 160.—*Some in their horse.* That is, their horses, the word here being plural. Plurals and possessives of nouns ending in *s*-sounds were often written without the additional syllable in the time of Shakespeare. Cf. *King John*, ii. 1. 289: "Sits on his horse back at mine hostess' door"; *Merchant of Venice*, iv. 1. 255: "Are there balance here to weigh the flesh?" etc.

Page 163.—*William Kemp dancing the Morris*. Kemp was a favorite comic actor in the latter years of the reign of Elizabeth. He acted in some of Shakespeare's plays and in some of Ben Jonson's, when they were first put upon the stage. In 1599 he journeyed from London to Norwich, dancing the Morris all the way. The next year he published an account of the exploit, entitled *The Nine daies wonder*. The cut here is a fac-simile of one on the title-page of this pamphlet. It represents Kemp, with his attendant, Tom the Piper, playing on the pipe and tabor. They spent four weeks on the journey, nine days of which were occupied in the dancing. At Chelmsford the crowd assembled to receive them was so great that they were an hour in making their way through it to their lodgings. At this town "a maid not passing fourteen years of age" challenged Kemp to dance the Morris with her "in a great large room," and held out a whole hour, at the end of which he was "ready to lie down" from exhaustion. On another occasion a "lusty country lass" wanted to try her skill with him, and "footed it merrily to Melford, being a long mile." Between Bury and Thetford he performed the ten miles in three hours. On portions of the journey the roads were very bad, and his dancing was frequently interrupted by the hospitality or importunity of the people along the route. At Norwich he was received as an honored guest by the mayor of the city.

Page 168.—*Corresponded to our 3d of May*. The difference between Old and New Style in reckoning dates, and the fact that the Gregorian Calendar (or New Style) was not adopted in England until 1752, or nearly two hundred years after it was accepted by Catholic nations on the Continent, have often led historians, biographers, and other writers into mistakes concerning dates in the 16th, 17th, and 18th centuries. For instance, it has been often asserted that Shakespeare and the Spanish dramatist Cervantes died on the same day, April 23, 1616; but Shakespeare actually died ten days later than his great contemporary, New Style having been adopted in Spain in 1582. If we were certain that Shakespeare was born on the 23d of April, 1564, we ought now to celebrate the anniversary of his birth on the 3d of May. As we do not know the precise date of his birth, and the 23d of April has come to be generally recognized as the anniversary, there is no particular reason for changing it.

Richard Johnson. He was born in 1573 and died about 1659. He is chiefly noted as the author of this *Famous History of the Seven Champions of Christendom.* These, according to him, were St. George of England, St. Denis of France, St. James of Spain, St. Antony of Italy, St. Andrew of Scotland, St. Patrick of Ireland, and St. David of Wales.

Mr. A. H. Wall, of Stratford-on-Avon, was for several years the librarian of the Shakespeare Memorial Library there, and is the author of many scholarly articles in English periodicals on subjects connected with Shakespeare and Warwickshire.

The Percy Reliques. A collection of old ballads, entitled *Reliques of Ancient English Poetry* (1765), made by Thomas Percy (1729–1811), a clergyman (in 1782 made Bishop of Dromore in Ireland) and poet.

Page 170. — *Chambers.* These are mentioned in more than one account of the burning of the Globe Theatre in London, on the 29th of June, 1613, when, as the critics generally agree, Shakespeare's *Henry VIII.* was the play being performed. A letter written by John Chamberlain to Sir Ralph Winwood, describing the fire, says that it "fell out by a peale of chambers," and a letter from Thomas Lorkin to Sir Thomas Puckering, dated "this last of June, 1613," says: "No longer since than yesterday, while Bourbege* his companie were acting at yᵉ Globe the play of Hen=8, and there shooting of certayne chambers in way of triumph, the fire catch'd." Another account states that these cannon were fired on King Henry's arrival at Cardinal Wolsey's house ; and the original stage-direction in *Henry VIII.* (iv. 1.) orders "chambers discharged" at the entrance of the king to the "mask at the cardinal's house."

Page 171.—*Ambrose Dudley.* He was born about 1530, made Earl of Warwick when Elizabeth came to the throne, and died in 1589.

Page 172. — *The Cage.* This house, on the corner of Fore Bridge Street (see map on page 42), was occupied by Thomas Quiney after he married Judith Shakespeare. "The house has

---

* Richard Burbage (1567?–1619) was a noted English actor. He made his fame at the Blackfriars and the Globe, of which he was a proprietor. He excelled in tragedy, and is said to have been the original Hamlet, Lear, and Othello. He was a painter as well as an actor. When this fire occurred at the Globe Theatre, he narrowly escaped with his life.

long been modernized, the only existing portions of the ancient building being a few massive beams supporting the floor over the cellar " (Halliwell-Phillipps).

Page 173.—*Sir Thomas Browne* (1605–1682) was an eminent physician and author. Among his books were the *Religio Medici* (1643), *Vulgar Errors* (1646), etc.

Sir John Suckling (baptized Feb. 10, 1609, and supposed to have died by suicide at Paris about 1642) was a Royalist poet in the Court of Charles I. He wrote some plays, but is best known by his minor poems, one of the most noted of which is the *Ballad upon a Wedding*.

Page 174.—*Izaak Walton* (1593–1683) is famous as the author of *The Complete Angler* (1653), one of the classics of our literature. He also wrote Lives of Donne, Hooker, Herbert, and other English divines.

Richard Hooker (1553?–1600) was a celebrated theologian, author of *Laws of Ecclesiastical Polity*, four books of which appeared in 1592, a fifth in 1597, and the remaining three after his death.

Page 180. — *Warner's Albion's England.* William Warner (1558?–1609) was the author of *Albion's England* (1586), a rhymed history of the country, and the translator of the *Menæchmi* of the Latin dramatist Plautus (1595), on which Shakespeare founded the plot of the *Comedy of Errors*.

Page 182.—*Watchet-colored.* Light blue. Compare Spenser, *F. Q.* iii. 4. 40: " Their watchet mantles frindgd with silver rownd."

Like a wild Morisco. That is, a morris-dancer. The quotation is from 2 *Henry VI.* iii. 1. 365 :—

> " I have seen
> Him caper upright like a wild Morisco,
> Shaking the bloody darts as he his bells."

Page 183. — *The featliest of dancers.* The most dexterous. Compare *The Winter's Tale*, iv. 4. 176 : " She dances featly " ; and *The Tempest*, i. 2. 380 : " Foot it featly," etc.

William Browne (1591–1643 ?) published book i. of *Britannia's Pastorals* in 1613. He also wrote *The Shepherd's Pipe* (1614) and other poems.

Page 184.—*A carved hook*, that is, a shepherd's crook (called a " sheep-hook " in *The Winter's Tale*, iv. 4. 431), as the *scrip* is his pouch or wallet. Compare *As You Like It* (iii. 2. 171), where Touchstone says to Corin : " Come, shepherd, let us make an honourable retreat ; though not with bag and baggage, yet with scrip and scrippage."

John Aubrey (1626–1697), besides assisting Anthony Wood in his *Antiquities of Oxford* (1674), wrote *Miscellanies*, a collection of short stories and other tales of the supernatural.

Page 185.—*The Puritan Stubbes.* Concerning this Philip Stubbes little appears to be known except that he was educated at Oxford and Cambridge, but became a rigid Puritan, and wrote several books besides the famous *Anatomie of Abuses.*

Richard Carew (1555–1620) was a poet and antiquarian, and for a time high sheriff of Cornwall.

Page 186. —*Pageants.* The word in Shakespeare's day was generally applied to theatrical entertainments.

Play the woman's part. Female parts were played by boys or young men until after the middle of the 17th century. Samuel Pepys, in his *Diary*, under date of January 3, 1660, writes : " To the Theatre, where was acted ' Beggar's Brush,' it being very well done ; and here the first time that ever I saw women come upon the stage." Again, under February 12, 1660, he records a performance of *The Scornful Lady*, adding : " now done by a woman, which makes the play appear much better than ever it did to me."

Made her weep a-good. That is, heartily.

Passioning. Grieving, lamenting. Compare *Venus and Adonis*, 1059 : " Dumbly she passions," etc.

Page 190. — *Steevens.* George Steevens (1736–1800) was an eccentric but accomplished editor and critic. " He was often wantonly mischievous, and delighted to stumble for the mere gratification of dragging unsuspicious innocents into the mire with him. He was, in short, the very Puck of commentators."

John Heywood (1500 ?–1580) was a dramatist and epigrammatist. His interludes " prepared the way for English comedy," the characters having some individuality instead of being mere walking virtues and vices. Of these plays *The Four P's* (printed between 1543 and 1547) is the best known. The characters that give it the name are a Palmer, a Pardoner, a Potecary (apothecary) and a Pedlar. A *palmer* was a pilgrim to the Holy Land, so called from the palm-branch he brought back in token of having performed the journey, A *pardoner* was a person licensed to sell papal indulgences, or *pardons.*

No night is now, etc. The quotation is from *A Midsummer-Night's Dream*, ii. 1. 102.

Page 191.—*Housen.* An obsolete plural of *house*, formed like *oxen*, etc.

Page 192.—*The offices.* The rooms in an old English mansion where provisions are kept ; that is, the pantry, kitchen, etc.

Waes-hael. Anglo-Saxon for "Be hale (whole, or well)," equivalent to "Here's to your health." *Wassail* is a corruption of this salutation, which from this meaning was transferred to festive gatherings where it was used, and then to the liquor served on such occasions—generally, spiced ale.

The tenant of Ingon. When Knight wrote this, fifty or more years ago, he supposed that a certain John Shakespeare who in 1570 held a farm known as *Ingon* or *Ington*, in the parish of Hampton Lucy near Stratford, was the poet's father ; but that he was one of the many other Shakespeares in Warwickshire (see page 207 below) appears from an entry in the parish register at Hampton Lucy, showing that he was buried on the 25th of September, 1589. The poet's father lived until September, 1601, his funeral being registered as having taken place on the 8th of that month. There was another John Shakespeare, a shoemaker, who was a resident of Stratford from about 1584 to about 1594. In the town records he is generally called the "shumaker," or "corvizer" (an obsolete word of the same meaning), or "cordionarius" (the Latin equivalent) ; but occasionally he appears simply as "John Shakspere," and some of these entries were formerly supposed to refer to the father of the dramatist.

The Lord of Misrule. The person chosen to direct the Christmas sports and revels. His sovereignty lasted during the twelve days of the holiday season. Stow, in his *Survey of London* (see on page 82 above), says : "In the feast of Christmas, there was in the king's house, wheresoever he lodged, a Lord of Misrule, or Master of Merry Disports, and the like had ye in the house of every nobleman of honour or good worship, were he spiritual or temporal." Stubbes (see on page 185 above) inveighed against the practice in his usual bitter way : "First, all the wild heads of the parish, conventing together, choose them a grand captain (of mischief) whom they innoble with the title of my Lord of Misrule, and him they crown with great solemnity, and adopt for their king. This king anointed chooseth forth twenty, forty, three score, or a hundred lusty guts like to himself, to wait upon his lordly majesty, and to guard his noble person. Then every one of these his men he investeth with his liveries, of green, yellow, or some other light wanton color. . . . And they have their hobby-

horses, dragons, and other antics, together with their bawdy pipers
and thundering drummers, to strike up the devil's dance withal ;
. . . and in this sort they go to the church (though the minister
be at prayer or preaching) dancing and swinging their handkerchiefs over their heads in the church, like devils incarnate, with
such a confused noise that no man can hear his own voice. . . .
Then after this, about the church they go again and again, and so
forth into the churchyard, where they have commonly their summer halls, their bowers, arbors, and banqueting houses set up,
wherein they feast, banquet, and dance all that day, and (peradventure) all that night too. And thus these terrestrial furies spend
their Sabbath day." He goes on to tell how the people give money,
food, and drink for these festivities, and adds : " but if they knew
that, as often as they bring any to the maintenance of these exe-
crable pastimes, they offer sacrifice to the Devil and Sathanas
[Satan], they would repent, and withdraw their hands, which God
grant they may." The Lords of Misrule in colleges were preached
against at Cambridge by the Puritans in the reign of James I. as
inconsistent with a place of religious education, and as a relic of
Pagan worship. In Scotland, the "Abbot of Unreason" (as the
Lord of Misrule was called there), with other festive characters,
was suppressed by legislation as early as 1555. Thomas Fuller
(1608–1681), in his *Good Thoughts in Worse Times* (1647), says :
" Some sixty years since, in the University of Cambridge, it was
solemnly debated betwixt the heads [of the colleges] to debar
young scholars of that liberty allowed them in Christmas, as inconsistent with the discipline of students. But some grave gover-
nors mentioned the good use thereof, because thereby, in twelve
days, they more discover the dispositions of scholars than in twelve
months before."

Page 193.— *The Clopton who is gone*. William Clopton, whose
tomb is in the north aisle of Stratford Church He was the father
of the William Clopton of Shakespeare's boyhood, who resided at
Clopton House, an ancient mansion less than two miles from Stratford on the brow of the Welcombe Hills. It is still standing,
though long ago modernized. It is said to have been originally
surrounded with a moat, like the "moated grange" of *Measure for
Measure* (iii. I. 277).

To burn this night with torches. That is, to prolong the festivities. The quotation is from *Antony and Cleopatra*, iv. 2. 41.

John Dyer (1700–1758) was an English poet, author of *Grongar
Hill* (1727), *The Ruins of Rome* (1740), etc.

CLOPTON MONUMENTS

Page 194.—*Flawns.* A kind of custard-pie. Compare Ben Jonson, *Sad Shepherdess*, i. 2 :—

> " Fall to your cheese-cakes, curds, and clouted cream,
> Your fools, your flawns," etc.

The *fools* were also a kind of custard, or fruit with whipped cream, etc. *Gooseberry-fool* is still an English dish.

Page 195.—*The cost of the sheep-shearing feast.* Mr. Knight makes a little slip here. The Clown, on his way to buy materials for the feast, tries to reckon up mentally what the *wool* from the shearing will bring. " Let me see," he says ; " every 'leven wether tods [that is, yields a *tod*, or 28 pounds of wool] ; every tod yields pound and odd shilling ; fifteen hundred shorn,—what comes the wool to ?" Then, after vainly attempting to make out what the amount will be, he adds : " I cannot do 't without counters" (round pieces of metal used in reckoning), and, giving up the problem, turns to considering what he is to buy for his sister : " Let me see ; what am I to buy for our sheep-shearing feast ? Three pound of sugar, five pound of currants, rice,—what will this sister of mine do with rice ? But my father hath made her mistress of the feast, and she lays it on. She hath made me four-and-twenty nosegays for the shearers, — three-man songmen all, and very good ones ; but they are most of them means and bases ; but one Puritan amongst them, and he sings psalms to hornpipes. I must have saffron to colour the warden pies ; mace, dates—none ; that's out of my note : nutmegs, seven ; a race or two of ginger,—but that I may beg ; four pound of prunes, and as many of raisins o' the sun." *Three-man songmen* are singers of catches in three parts. *Means* are tenors. *Warden pies* are pies made of *wardens,* a kind of large pears, which were usually baked or roasted. A *race* of ginger is a root of it ; and *raisins o' the sun* are raisins dried in the sun.

Page 196. — *Paul Hentzner.* He was a native or Silesia (1558–1623) who wrote a *Journey through Germany, France, Italy,* etc.

Matthew Stevenson wrote several other books in prose and verse, published between 1654 and 1673.

The furmenty-pot. The word *furmenty* is a corruption of *frumenty* (see page 197), which is derived from the Latin *frumentum,* meaning wheat. The hulled wheat, boiled in milk and seasoned, was a popular dish in England, as it still is in the rural districts.

Robert Herrick (1591–1674) was an English lyric poet. The *Hesperides* was his most important work. A complete edition of his poems, edited by Mr. Grosart, was published in 1876.

Page 197. — *A mawkin.* A kitchen-wench, or other menial servant. The word is only a phonetic spelling of *malkin*, which Shakespeare has in *Coriolanus*, ii. 1. 224: "the kitchen malkin." Compare Tennyson, *The Princess*, v. 25 :—

> ' If this be he,—or a draggled mawkin, thou,
>   That tends her bristled grunters in the sludge;

that is, a female swineherd.

Prank them up. Adorn themselves.

The fill-horse. The word *fill*, for the *thills* or shafts of a vehicle, used by Shakespeare and other writers of that day, is now obsolete in England, though still current in New England. *Cross* means to make the sign of the cross upon or over the animal.

Page 199. — *Sheffield whittles.* Knives made at Sheffield. Chaucer, in the *Canterbury Tales* (3931) refers to a "Shefeld thwitel," or whittle. Compare Shakespeare, *Timon of Athens*, v. 1. 173: "There's not a whittle in the unruly camp," etc.

Rings with posies. Rings with mottoes inscribed inside them. *Posy* is the same word as *poesy*, which we also find used in this sense. Compare *Hamlet*, iii. 2. 162: "Is this a prologue, or the poesy of a ring?" The fashion of putting such posies on rings prevailed from the middle of the 16th century to the close of the 17th. In 1624 a little book was published with the title, *Love's Garland, or Posies for Rings, Handkerchiefs, and Gloves; and such pretty tokens, that lovers send their loves.* Compare page 53 above.

Page 201. — *Qui est la?* Who is there? (French). The reply is, "Peasants, poor French people."

Whipped three market-days. For some petty offence he had committed.

Page 202. — *Wick-yarn.* For making wicks for the oil-lamps then in common use. It was a familiar article in this country fifty years ago, when whale-oil was used for household illumination.

Napery. Linen for domestic use, especially table-linen.

Inkles, caddises, coifs, stomachers, pomanders, etc. All these things are found in the peddler's pack of Autolycus in *The Winter's Tale* (iv. 4). Compare page 204 below. *Caddises* are worsted ribbons, or galloons. *Inkles* are a kind of tape. *Pomanders* were little balls made of perfumes, and worn in the pocket or about the neck, for the sake of the fragrance or as a mere ornament, and sometimes to prevent infection in times of plague.

The ivy-bush. A bush or tuft of ivy was in olden time the sign of a vintner. Compare the cut of the Morris Dance, opposite page 178. The old proverb, " Good wine needs no bush" (*As You Like It*, v. epil.), means that a place where good wine is kept needs no sign to attract customers. Gascoigne, in his *Glass of Government* (1575), says: " Now a days the good wyne needeth none ivye garland."

Page 203.—*The juggler with his ape.* The ape being used to perform tricks, as monkeys are nowadays by organ-grinders to amuse their street audiences. In *The Winter's Tale* (iv. 3. 101) the Clown says of Autolycus: " I know this man well . he hath been since an ape-bearer"; that is, he carried round a trained ape as a show.

Cantabanqui. Strolling ballad-singers ; literally, persons who sing upon a bench (from the Italian *catambanco*, formerly *cantinbanco*). Compare Sir Henry Taylor, *Philip van Artevelde*, i. 3. 2 :—

> " He was no tavern cantabank that made it,
> But a squire minstrel of your Highness' court."

The Tale of Sir Topas. One of Chaucer's *Canterbury Tales*, *The Rime of Sir Topas*, a burlesque upon the metrical romances of the time. It is written in ballad form.

Bevis of Southampton. A fabulous hero of the time of William the Conqueror. He is mentioned in *Henry VIII.* i. 1. 38 :—

> " that former fabulous story,
> Being now seen possible enough, got credit,
> That Bevis was believed;"

that is, *so* that the old romantic legend became credible. In 2 *Henry VI.*, after the words (ii. 3. 89), " have at thee with a down-right blow," some editors add from the old play on which this is founded : "as Bevis of Southampton fell upon Ascapart," a giant whom he was said to have conquered. Figures of Bevis and Ascapart formerly adorned the Bar-gate at Southampton, as shown in the cut on the next page ; but when the gate was repaired some years ago they were removed to the museum.

Adam Bell and Clymme of the Clough (that is, of the Cliff) figure in a popular old ballad, which may be found in Percy's *Reliques.*

16

The woolen statute-caps. Caps which, by Act of Parliament in 1571, the citizens were required to wear on Sundays and holidays. The nobility were exempt from the requirement, which, as Strype informs us, was "in behalf of the trade of cappers"—one of sundry such "protection" measures in the time of Elizabeth. Compare *Love's Labour's Lost*, v. 2. 282: "Well, better wits have worn plain statute-caps." As Knight intimates here, the law was a very unpopular one.

THE BAR-GATE, SOUTHAMPTON

The Wife of Bath's husbands. Alluding to the *Wife of Bath*, one of Chaucer's Canterbury pilgrims. In the prologue to her tale, she says of her husbands (of whom she had five in succession):—

> "I governed hem so wel after my lawe,
>   That eche of hem ful blisful was and fawe [fain, or glad]
>   To bringen me gay things fro the feyre."

That is, as she goes on to explain, they were glad to bring her presents from the fair to keep her in good humor, as otherwise she was apt to treat them "spitously," or spitefully.

Where a coxcomb will be broke. That is, a head will be broken ;

but it should be understood that this does not mean a fractured skull, but merely a bruise sufficient to break the skin and make the blood flow. Shakespearian critics have sometimes misapprehended this and similar expressions. In *Romeo and Juliet* (i. 2. 52), where the hero says, "Your plantain-leaf is excellent for that" (referring to a "broken shin"), Ulrici, the eminent German commentator, thinks that he must be speaking ironically, as plantain "was used to stop the blood, but not for a fracture of a bone." Compare *Twelfth Night*, v. 1. 178, where Sir Andrew says: "He has broke my head across and has given Sir Toby a bloody coxcomb too."

Page 206. — *Junkets.* The word here means sweetmeats or delicacies.

Properties. In the theatrical sense of stage requisites, such as costumes and other equipments and appointments.

Incurious. Not *curious*, in the original sense of *careful;* not fastidious, and therefore pleased with these inferior actors.

And possess. The subject of *possess* is omitted, after the loose fashion of the time, being obviously implied in *rustics.* Compare *Hamlet*, iii. 1. 8 :—

> "Nor do we find him forward to be sounded,
> But with a crafty madness keeps aloof";

that is, *he* keeps aloof.

Page 207. — *We see not its workings.* We see the results, but not the processes by which they have been brought about.

The "green lap" in which the boy poet was "laid." The quotations are from the passage referring to Shakespeare in *The Progress of Poesy* by Thomas Gray (1716–1771) :—

> "Far from the sun and summer gale,
> In thy green lap was Nature's darling laid,
> What time, where lucid Avon stray'd,
> To him the mighty mother did unveil
> Her awful face ' the dauntless child
> Stretch'd forth his little arms and smil'd.
> 'This pencil take,' she said, ' whose colors clear
> Richly paint the vernal year:
> Thine too these golden keys, immortal boy!
> This can unlock the gates of joy;
> Of horror that, and thrilling fears,
> Or ope the sacred fount of sympathetic tears.'"

The name of Shakespeare was very common. See note on *The tenant of Ingon*, page 192, above.

Page 208.—*Volumes have been written on the plant-lore*, etc. The best of these is Rev. H. N. Ellacombe's *Plant-Lore and Garden-craft of Shakespeare*, which is quoted on the next page.

Apricocks. An old form of *apricots*.

Page 209.—*In the compass of a pale.* Within the limits of an enclosure, or walled garden.

Knots. Interlacing beds. Compare Milton, *P. L.* iv. 242 : "In beds and curious knots"; and *Love's Labour 's Lost*, i. 1. 249 : "thy curious-knotted garden."

He that hath suffer'd, etc. King Richard.

At time of year. That is, at the proper season.

Confound itself. Ruin or destroy itself. Compare *The Merchant of Venice*, iii. 2. 278 :—

> " Never did I know
> A creature that did bear the shape of man
> So keen and greedy to confound a man."

Page 210.—*To prove his real profession.* Books and essays have been written to prove Shakespeare's intimate knowledge of various professions and occupations—law, medicine, military science, seamanship, etc.

ADDENDA

Page 21.—*The letters E. R.* Young readers may need to be informed that these letters stand for *Elizabeth Regina* (Latin for *Queen*).

Page 37.—*The elder Robert of Stratford.* Sidney Lee says : " Robert, the father of the prelates Robert and John, was a well-to-do inhabitant of Stratford, who appears to have set his sons an example in local works of benevolence. He it is to whom has been attributed the foundation, in 1296, of the chapel of the guild, and of the hospital or almshouses attached to it."

Page 59.—*Old House on High Street.* This house, the finest example of Elizabethan architecture in Stratford, and one of the best in England, was built in 1596 by Thomas Rogers, whose daughter, Katherine, married Robert Harvard, a butcher in the parish of St. Saviour in London, and became the mother of John Harvard, the early benefactor of Harvard College from whom it took its name. The house of Thomas Rogers was nearly opposite

New Place, the residence of Shakespeare in his later years; and Mr. Rogers and his daughter doubtless knew the dramatist as a famous neighbor of theirs, and may have seen him on the stage. The cut on page 59 gives no adequate idea of the elaborate carving on the front; but this is well shown in the full-page heliotype in Mr. Henry F. Waters's *Genealogical Gleanings in England*, where these facts concerning the parentage of John Harvard first appeared. On the front of the house, under the second-story window, is the inscription,

TR   1596   AR

The "AR" doubtless stands for Alice Rogers, the second wife of Thomas. This proves that the second marriage occurred before 1596. Mr. Waters found no record of the burial of the first wife, Margaret, but that of Alice was on the 17th of August, 1608, and that of her husband on the 20th of February, 1610–11. The Globe Theatre, of which Shakespeare was a shareholder, stood in the parish of St. Saviour. Robert Harvard died in 1625, and was buried in St. Saviour's Church. His widow appears to have been married twice (to John Elletson and Richard Yearwood) before her death in 1635; but the date of the Elletson marriage (Jan. 19, 1625) given by Mr. Waters cannot be correct if that of Robert Harvard's death (Aug. 24, 1625) is right.

Page 89.—*Adonai or Elohim.* Hebrew names for Jehovah, or God.

Page 112.—*Shrewd turns.* That is, evil turns (chances or happenings). Cf. *Henry VIII.* v. 3. 176:—

> "The common voice, I see, is verified
> Of thee, which says thus, 'Do my Lord of Canterbury
> A shrewd turn, and he is your friend for ever';"

that is, he returns good for evil. Compare *As You Like It*, v. 4. 178:—

> "And after, every [every one] of this happy number
> That have endur'd shrewd days and nights with us
> Shall share the good of our returned fortune;"

and Chaucer, *Tale of Melibæus:* "The prophete saith: Flee shrewdnesse, and do goodnesse," etc.

Page 162.—*A sergeant at-arms his mace.* In Old English *his* was often put in this way after proper names, which had no genitive (or possessive) inflection. In the 16th century it came to be used frequently in place of the possessive ending *-s*. It was occasionally used in the 17th and 18th centuries, when some grammarians adopted the false theory that the possessive ending was a contraction of *his*. The construction occurs now and then in Shakespeare; as in *Twelfth Night*, iii. 3. 26: "the count his galleys," etc.

Page 191.—*An age of music.* Such was the Elizabethan age. Shakespeare himself had a hearty love of music, and evidently a good knowledge of the science, as the many allusions to it in his works abundantly prove. No less than thirty two of the plays contain interesting references to music and musical matters in the text; and there are also over three hundred stage-directions of a musical nature scattered through thirty-six of the plays. Mr. Edward W. Naylor, in his *Shakespeare and Music* (London, 1896), says: "We find that in the 16th and 17th centuries a practical acquaintance with music was a regular part of the education of the sovereign, gentlemen of rank, and the higher middle class. . . . There is plenty of evidence that the lower classes were as enthusiastic about music as the higher. A large number of passages in contemporary authors show clearly that singing in parts (especially of 'catches') was a common amusement with blacksmiths, colliers, cloth-workers, cobblers, tinkers, watchmen, country-parsons, and soldiers. . . . If ever a country deserved to be called musical, that country was England in the 16th and 17th centuries. King and courtier, peasant and ploughman, each could 'take his part,' with each music was a part of his daily life. . . . In this respect, at any rate, the 'good old days' were indeed better than those we now see. Even a *public-house song* in Elizabeth's day was a canon in three parts, a thing which could only be managed first time through' nowadays by the very first rank of professional singers."

Page 204.—*Sweet hearts.* This must not be supposed to be a misprint for *Sweethearts*, which was originally two words and often used as a tender or affectionate address. *Sweetheart* occurs in Shakespeare only in *The Winter's Tale*, iv. 4. 664: "take your sweetheart's hat," etc.

INDEX

ARMS OF JOHN SHAKESPEARE

Date Due